BRAND'
BRA
1300
WILMINGTON, DE 19803

MW00997713

Modern Critical Interpretations

Shakespeare's Sonnets

Modern Critical Interpretations

These and other titles in preparation

Shakespeare's
Sonnets

Edited and with an introduction by

Harold Bloom
Sterling Professor of the Humanities
Yale University

Chelsea House Publishers

NEW YORK ◊ PHILADELPHIA

© 1987 by Chelsea House Publishers,
a subsidiary of Haights Cross Communications.

Introduction © 1987 by Harold Bloom

Printed and bound in the United States of America

10 9 8 7

∞ The paper used in this publication meets the minimum
requirements of the American National Standard for
Permanence of Paper for Printed Library Materials, Z39.48-
1984.

Library of Congress Cataloging-in-Publication Data
Shakespeare's sonnets.
    (Modern critical interpretations)
    Bibliography: p.
    Includes index.
    Summary: A collection of six critical essays on the sonnets of
Shakespeare, arranged in chronological order of original
publication.
    1. Shakespeare, William, 1564–1616. Sonnets.
2. Sonnets, English—History and criticism.
[1. Shakespeare, William, 1564–1616.   Sonnets.
2. Sonnets—History and criticism]   I. Bloom, Harold.
II. Series.
PP2848.S46   1987   821 ′ .3
87–8091
ISBN 0–87754–938–9

Contents

Editor's Note

This volume gathers together a representative selection of the best modern criticism of Shakespeare's Sonnets. The critical essays are reprinted here in the chronological order of their original publication. I am grateful to Patricia Phillippy for her aid in editing this volume.

My introduction analyzes Sonnet 94, finding in it considerably fewer ambivalences than generally are found, and connecting it to elements in Hamlet's character and Othello's fate. C. L. Barber's essay on the Sonnets begins the chronological sequence by suggesting that Shakespeare confronted his own nature in these poems, and thus learned how to represent "the transformation of suffering into compassion."

In Rosalie L. Colie's reading, the Sonnets invite us to become critics, and so to see "how a man's fundamental moral existence can be a matter of style." More formalistically and historically, as befits the most reliable commentator the Sonnets have yet enjoyed, Stephen Booth explores three crucial poems, Sonnets 116, 129, and 146.

Thomas M. Greene, in an exegesis that seeks to restore force to our waning Humanism, finds in the Sonnets a vision of "a radical flaw in the universe, in emotion, in value, and in language," a flaw the Sonnets make considerable effort to compensate.

In this volume's final essay, Howard Felperin presents a comprehensive view of how a deconstructionist criticism could undertake the project of properly reading Shakespeare's Sonnets. Felperin's epigraph, from T. S. Eliot, is the apt motto to Felperin's essay and to the other essays in this book, the introduction included. Shakespeare is so strong that we are bound to misread him. From time to time we ought to "change our way of being wrong," and so give the Sonnets, and the rest of Shakespeare, what I myself would want to call strong misreadings rather than merely weak and repetitious misreadings.

Introduction

Is there an equivalent in Shakespeare's Sonnets to his most original power as a dramatist: to represent changes in his characters as ensuing from their overhearing of what they themselves say, whether to others or to themselves? Does the condensed art of a sonnet allow Shakespeare to become one of his own characters, as it were, caught in the process of changing as a reaction to, or reflection of, his own utterance? I do not mean to ask again how dramatic the Sonnets are or are not. Rather, I wonder if any among the Sonnets fulfill A. D. Nuttall's fine assertion for Shakespearean mimesis, that it makes us see aspects of reality we never could have seen without it.

The aesthetic strength of the Sonnets has little to do with their appearance in a sequence, as more seems to be lost than gained when we read them straight through in order. As a rough series of isolated splendors, the best among them are rightly judged to be the most eminent in the language, superior not only to Spenser, Sidney, and Drayton, but also to Milton, Wordsworth, and Keats. They have a monumental quality difficult to match in any Western language, worthy of the poet of "The Phoenix and the Turtle."

Not many critics have preferred Sonnet 94 to all the other sonnets, but it has intrigued nearly every commentator because of its ambivalences:

> They that have pow'r to hurt, and will do none,
> That do not do the thing they most do show,
> Who moving others, are themselves as stone,
> Unmoved, cold, and to temptation slow,
> They rightly do inherit heaven's graces,
> And husband nature's riches from expense;
> They are the lords and owners of their faces,

1

Others but stewards of their excellence.
The summer's flow'r is to the summer sweet,
Though to itself it only live and die,
But if that flow'r with base infection meet,
The basest weed outbraves his dignity:
   For sweetest things turn sourest by their deeds;
   Lilies that fester smell far worse than weeds.

Stephen Booth sees this as "a stylistic mirror of the speaker's indecision," and observes that "The sentences wander from attribute to attribute in such a way that a reader's response to 'them' who are the subject of lines 1–8 swings repeatedly back and forth between negative and positive." The crucial question then would be: Is the speaker's indecision resolved through the implications of the couplet ending the poem? But that in turn depends upon another question: how undecided truly is the speaker in regard to "them"?

If you choose not to hurt someone else, even as your outward semblance intimates you almost certainly are about to do so, there may be a considerable touch of sadomasochism in you. Or you may be like Hamlet, who most provokes the love of the audience in act 5, where he is beyond the reach of love. An unmoved mover is more a divinity than a magnet, and so rightly inherits heaven's graces. So far at least the poem that I encounter is no mirror of its speaker's supposed indecision.

To "husband nature's riches from expense" *may* mean to hold one's sexuality in reserve, to abstain from expending it, but I am reluctant, in the context of Sonnet 94, to so restrict the sense of "nature's riches." We think of Hamlet as one of nature's great treasures because we think of him as an adventure of and in the spirit. In act 5, he manifests extraordinary disinterestedness; are we so far from that Hamlet if we speak of him as husbanding nature's riches from expense? In full and final control, the Hamlet of act 5 indeed is the lord and owner of his face, the outward image that he turns to Elsinore and to the audience. That brings us to the puzzling line: "Others but stewards of their excellence," where the emphasis upon "their" clearly gives us not "others" but "lords and owners" as the antecedent. To continue with my *Hamlet* analogue, Horatio is a prime instance of one of those stewards of excellence, who survive to tell the story of the greater figures they admire and love.

On this reading, the hero, Hamlet or another, is "the summer's flow'r," sweet to Horatio and the audience, but essentially living and dying by and for himself, for ends we can only partly apprehend, let alone accept. The crisis of meaning turns upon the nature of the base infection that the hero meets. I do not accept a reading that associates the infection with the weed, for the "base" in "base infection" means "debasing" or potentially debasing, whereas "the basest weed" is already debased. Think of poor Othello as summer's flower debased by the infection of jealous madness, and so fallen into the terrible lack of dignity of his madness at its incoherent worst. Hamlet is precisely a being who is not turned sourest by his deeds, not a lily that festers.

I hardly seek to turn the Sonnets (1592 to 1596, or so) into a prophecy of *Hamlet* (1600 to 1601) or rather say of *Othello* (1604), but Sonnet 94 is emblematic of the tragedian who was to come, unless indeed it was written later than most of the other sonnets, which is possible enough. On my reading, it is the negative equivalent of what Wordsworth celebrated when he chanted that feeling comes in aid of feeling, and diversity of strength attends us if but once we have been strong. Strength, in Shakespeare, becomes horror when feeling comes to prey upon feeling, and Othello or Macbeth fall into ruin the more dreadfully because, in their different ways, they were so strong.

I do not find then the ambivalences in Sonnet 94 that so many, including Empson, have found, and so I do not find the speaker changing in the final couplet. I would suppose then that the Sonnets, even at their strongest, are indeed lyric rather than dramatic, marvelously conventional rather than personally expressive. Wordsworth and Keats learn from Shakespeare in their sonnets, but are closer to Milton because they put into their sonnets, as Milton sometimes did, the burden of their prophecy. Shakespeare, who had the power to hurt, nevertheless husbanded nature's riches from expense in his Sonnets and chose rather to live and die not only to himself, in his tragedies.

An Essay on Shakespeare's Sonnets

C. L. Barber

Everyone who reads poetry knows a number of Shakespeare's Sonnets well, but many readers have been put off from the whole collection by the biographical questions it raises and the accumulation of unsatisfactory answers proposed by commentators. The Sonnets not only include some of the most beautiful poems ever written, but they have the additional interest that they are the only poems we have which Shakespeare wrote out of his own life, in his own person—a remarkable, indeed astonishing collection. People often wish that a diary or correspondence might turn up from which we could learn about Shakespeare; in the Sonnets we have, by a fluke, something of this kind. But they are cast in the mold of his age, not ours, and they do not oblige our curiosity about circumstantial facts. The *who, where, when* are beyond knowing, despite the tantalizing closeness of the poems to Shakespeare's personal life. The many theories that have been proposed were all expertly reviewed in 1944, in the hundreds of pages of the New Variorum Edition, by the late Professor Hyder Rollins, a master of objective literary scholarship; his conclusion was that "nothing worthy of the name of 'evidence' has been produced to substantiate any of them, and probably nothing ever will be" (*Sonnets,* 1951). Yet this barren tradition of biographical speculation has led many to assume—even when they see no answer—that *the* question about the Sonnets is "What is the story be-

From *The Laurel Shakespeare: The Sonnets.* ©1960 by Western Printing and Lithographing Co. Dell, 1960.

hind them?" The poems are usually discussed not as poems but as evidence—and insufficient evidence at that.

People who care about poetry usually react to this tendency by making a point of ignoring all questions as to what the Sonnets express of Shakespeare's life and attending only to what they are as autonomous poetic achievements. Shakespeare, in finding words for his love, often evokes what is loveliest in the world at large:

Making a couplement of proud compare
With sun and moon, with earth and sea's rich gems,
With April's first-born flowers, and all things rare,
That heaven's air in this huge rondure hems.

(Sonnet 21)

Such sonnets are products of the brief golden age of English poetry when the magic of the simplest, most fundamental things could be conveyed in unforced words. The Sonnets are also, within their forthright form, among the most exquisitely wrought creations of sound and syllable in the language. Frequently they give compelling utterance to experiences everyone goes through in love—anguish, elation, joy, dismay; and they realize with directness and fullness basic conditions of existence which love has to confront—the fact of mortality, the separateness of human beings, their need of each other, the graces that come unsought and undeserved.

It is better to read the Sonnets for these universal values than to lose their poetry by turning them into riddles about Shakespeare's biography. But to block off consideration of what they mean as an expression of Shakespeare's own experience is a needless sacrifice, which leads in practice to ignoring those many sonnets which hinge on the stresses of the poet's personal life, and to losing an important part of the meaning and beauty of the whole collection. We can turn our backs on the unanswerable questions of fact, and read the poems not as tantalizing clues but as *expression* of a man's experience. When we do so, we find that, though they do not tell a story, they do express a personality. They are gestures of love, concern, disappointment, anger or disgust, profoundly and candidly conveyed. That we cannot know who was actually addressed does not prevent our feeling and understanding the gestures. What is communicated in this way is not, of course, "the whole truth about Shakespeare." The Sonnets are only Shakespeare at certain times in certain kinds of relations, with a young man or several young men (Sonnets 1–126), with a dark-complexioned married woman of loose morals (Sonnets 127–152). And in them we see Shakespeare only where he is living by writing poetry to people, rather than living in other ways. But within these limits, we do encounter his personality, and it is an extraordinary one. Shakespeare exhibits, like Keats, astonishing "negative capability." He realizes others with a selflessness or lack of self that is sometimes poignant, sometimes desperate, even ugly, sometimes sublime. To look at the Sonnets in relation to their author does not mean turning away from their qualities as poetry; on the contrary, the poems gain meaning and beauty—even the ones most familiar. We can see in them a great artist encountering, in love, the predicaments of his temperament and his part in life. And we can see what he loved, turned into the substance of poetry.

I. "His Sugared Sonnets among His Private Friends"

To read the Sonnets most effectually one must keep in view the place they had in the poet's life. They were not written for publication, but to present to friends, not written all together, but singly and in groups at intervals over several years. In 1598, a schoolmaster, Francis Meres, surveying current writing, praised Shakespeare as the time's leading dramatist and poet, listed his plays and his published narrative poems, and then referred to "his sugared sonnets among his private friends." Two sonnets (138 and 144) were appropriated for an anthology in 1599, but the other one hundred and fifty-two were not published until 1609, late in Shakespeare's life, long after most of them must have been written. This was the only edition, brought out by a marginal publisher, clearly without Shakespeare's permission or supervision. The cryptic dedication to "Mr. W. H." was the publisher's, not Shakespeare's. It seems likely that this one edition was soon suppressed, for in spite of Shakespeare's established fame there is almost no notice of the Sonnets in the decades following their appearance: in 1640 they were so little known that a publisher ventured to pretend that he was bringing out unpublished poems of Shakespeare in issuing a rearranged version of the 1609 text.

The writing of sonnets was a short-lived literary fashion in the 1590s, beginning with the posthumous publication of Sidney's *Astrophel and Stella* in 1591. Sonneteering was a polite accomplishment; Shakespeare makes game of the fashion in *Love's Labor's Lost,* where the elegant young lords "turn sonnet" when they turn from study to courting: they compose sonnets, recite them, talk them, and finally forswear them as part and parcel of "spruce affectation." A number of sonnet sequences were published between 1592 and 1596 by Daniel, Watson, Drayton, Spenser and others; then the vogue was over. Shakespeare's Sonnets are often spoken of as his sonnet sequence, though they are not in fact such a production, indeed not one production at all. They were probably begun in the period when the rage for sonnets in private life was at its height, and when Shakespeare was making much of sonnets in his plays. There are a particularly large number of parallels in imagery and phrasing between the Sonnets, especially those numbered below one hundred, and *Love's Labor's Lost, Romeo and Juliet, A Midsummer Night's Dream, Richard II,* as well as the two narrative poems published in 1592 and 1594. These facts suggest that the bulk of the Sonnets were probably composed between 1593 and 1597. Many of them, however, including most of those numbered above one hundred in the collection, seem later in style, with affinities to the plays of the "problem" period, and so may have been composed later—unless, as some think, Shakespeare went through rapidly in the close form of the sonnet a development which came more slowly in the larger form of his plays.

C. S. Lewis has made the point that the typical Renaissance sonnet was a *public* form of poetry. "A good sonnet . . . was like a good public prayer: the test is whether the congregation can 'join' and make it their own, not whether it provides interesting materials for the spiritual biography of the compiler. The whole body of the sonnet sequences is more like an erotic liturgy than a series of erotic confidences" (*English Literature in the Sixteenth Century*). Many of Shakespeare's Sonnets are drastic (and unparalleled) exceptions to this rule: they refer to complicated and very private relations. But in his sonnets, as elsewhere, he uses the current idiom and goes beyond it or puts it to new uses rather than rebelling against it. He starts out with sonnets of ceremonial praise, seeking

> to say
> The perfect ceremony of love's rite.
>
> (Sonnet 23)

At intervals he makes astonishing explorations of passion, not because Shakespeare is telling a story, or writing a "confession," but because in living out his life he encounters complications which then become the subjects of sonnets. Occasionally the use of the sonnet as part of the poet's life seems to damage it as art—we sometimes sense distortion serving ulterior purposes, especially in the poems, addressed to the friend as patron, which seek to counter the bid for patronage of a rival poet (Sonnets 78–86). But an extraordinary honesty predominates.

II. The Sonnet as an Action

To read through the Sonnets at a sitting, though it is useful for surveying the topography they present, does violence to them and to the reader—it can produce a sensation of hothouse oppression. Each poem needs to be dwelt on; each requires the kind of concentrated attention which could have been given when they were received singly or in small groups. To read and reread is essential if we are to enjoy the way each moves, the use it makes of the possibilities of the sonnet form, the particular development in it of a design of sounds and images. The Sonnets ask for a special sort of attention because in them poetry is, in a special way, an action, something done for and to the beloved. Indeed sometimes the activity of the poetry alone makes endurable the passivity of the attitudes expressed by the poet.

Many of the Sonnets are wonderfully generous poems; they *give* meaning and beauty. The generosity is at once personal, a selfless love, and impersonal, the glow upon the world at the golden moment when Shakespeare began to write. The poems create a world resonant with the friend's beauty:

> Thou art thy mother's glass, and she in thee
> Calls back the lovely April of her prime;
> So thou through windows of thine age shalt see,
> Despite of wrinkles, this thy golden time.
>
> (Sonnet 3)

The curious theme of the first seventeen sonnets, which urge a friend to marry and have children, works partly because it provides occasions for saying simple things beautifully: how lovely April is; how fine it is that age, in spite of wrinkles, has windows through which to see its golden time renewed. The poet's vicarious interest in the young man's sexual fulfillment is not queasy because it is realized by evoking the creative power generally at work in nature:

> Those hours that with gentle work did frame
> The lovely gaze where every eye doth dwell.
>
> (Sonnet 5)

The phrase "gentle work" is typical of the direct cherishing of the processes of life. The feeling about the destructiveness of death is equally direct:

> For never-resting time leads summer on
> To hideous winter and confounds him there.
>
> (Sonnet 5)

There is no holding back from obvious words or metaphors: the sun's light is gracious, music is sweet, the buds of May are darling; death is winter, darkness, Time's scythe; beauty is all the usual things, for example a flower. But the meaning of the usual things is renewed:

> Since brass, nor stone, nor earth, nor boundless sea,
> But sad mortality o'ersways their power,
> How with this rage shall beauty hold a plea,
> Whose action is no stronger than a flower?
>
> (Sonnet 65)

That a flower is a fragile thing is familiar enough. But that a flower has its own kind of power too—this comes as a poignant realization. It often happens that the metaphorical vehicle in which Shakespeare conveys the tenor of his love absorbs our chief attention, so that the love itself is left behind or fulfilled in what it is compared to. We dwell on the fact that "summer's lease hath all too short a date," that the earth devours "her own sweet brood," that the morning flatters "the mountain tops with sovereign eye," that black night is "Death's second self," and "seals up all in rest." Consider, as a summary example, the direct descriptions of the seasons in Sonnets 97 and 98, "old December's bareness every where," "teeming autumn big with rich increase," "proud-pied April, dress'd in all his trim," and summer when we "wonder at the lily's white" and "praise the deep vermilion in the rose." The world is full of value that can be looked at front-face. Shakespeare could get more of this gold into his poetry than anyone else in the golden age because he had the greatest power of admiration.

To quote isolated phrases or lines from the Sonnets is unsatisfying, because every line or phrase is, in the act of reading, part of a single movement: when you know a sonnet well, an individual line, quoted alone, rings with the sound that it has in its proper place. Each sonnet is one utterance. Shakespeare's use of the form is simple and forthright and also delicate and subtle. He never varies from three quatrains followed by a couplet, *abab, cdcd, efef, gg:*

> Why write I still all one, ever the same,
> And keep invention in a noted weed,
> That every word doth almost tell my name?
> (Sonnet 76)

Other Elizabethan sonneteers showed more technical restlessness. Shakespeare not only uses nothing but the Shakespearean form (it *does* tell his name!), but for the most part he uses it straight. He does not run his syntax against the line endings or rhyme scheme. There are exceptions, but normally the sentences close with the close of each quatrain, or else are balanced symmetrically within the four-line unit. Within sentences, grammar and thought typically pause or turn at the end of the line; where they do run over, the enjambment is rarely emphatic. Shakespeare does not exploit the more outward forms of variation because within the pattern he is making astonishingly beautiful designs with sound and syllable and cadence. He is like an accomplished figure skater who sticks to the classical figures because what he cares about is what he can make of each evolution. (Shakespeare had, after all, unlimited opportunities in the plays for freestyle improvisations, swoops, spins, leaps.) Each sonnet is different, but the difference is achieved not by changing the framework of form but by moving in fresh ways within it.

It seems clear that Shakespeare wrote by quatrains. In coming to know a sonnet by heart, you find yourself recalling it one quatrain at a time and often getting stuck trying to move to the next, for lack of a tangible link. The imagery does not regularly carry through; what does carry through is the momentum of the discourse. The movement from quatrain to quatrain is usually a shift of some sort, though it can be simply a continuing with fresh impetus. The figure skater starts each evolution by kicking off from an edge, and can move from one evolution to another either by staying on the same edge of the same blade, or changing from inside edge to outside edge, or from left foot inside to right foot outside, and so on—each of these technical moves focusing a whole living gesture on the balancing, moving body. People praise Shakespeare's Sonnets because each one is about one thing: one should add that each is *one motion* about one thing, the motion normally being composed of three large sweeps and the shorter couplet. (The very different serial movement of Sonnet 66 is a revealing exception to prove the rule.)

It is important to recognize that in most of the Sonnets the couplet is *not* the emotional climax, or indeed even the musical climax; where it is made so, either by Shakespeare's leaning on it too heavily, or by our giving it unnecessary importance, one feels that two lines are asked to do too much. This let-down or overreach in the couplet is the most common defect in the Sonnets, though with tactful reading it usually can be kept from being troublesome. One needs to attend to the motion and the imaginative expansion which the sonnet achieves in the quatrains, realizing that the couplet is often no more than a turning around at the end to look from a new vantage at what has been expressed.

The main line of the sonnet as Shakespeare writes it is the patterned movement of discourse, not the imagery. The voice rides the undulation of the meter, gaining remarkable power and reaching out in ardent or urgent or solemn gestures defined by rhythmical variations. The criticism of our time has been fascinated by the way poetry can explore experience by carrying out the implications of a metaphor or conceit, as notably in Donne's work. Shakespeare in the Sonnets occasionally does something like this—most perfectly in the three paralleled metaphors of Sonnet 73: "That time of year . . . the twilight of such day . . . the glowing of such fire." But the progression by extending metaphors in Sonnet 73 is most definitely not typical. He is responsible to rhythmical, not metaphorical consistency. The sonnet often starts with something like a metaphorical program, but usually it is not carried through; metaphors are picked up, changed, mixed, dropped ad lib while the sonnet runs its strong course as an utterance.

One often finds, as one penetrates the poetic texture of a particular poem, that it holds together by determinate rhythm and sound several almost independent strains of meaning, or a cluster of ambiguities which, worked out logically, are almost mutually exclusive. A case in point, which also will be of interest to us in considering the relationship of Shakespeare to the friend he addresses, comes in Sonnet 16, where the poet urges that children can provide reproductions of the friend "much liker than your painted counterfeit," and then goes on with an extraordinarily rich use of the word "lines":

> So should the lines of life that life repair,
> Which this Time's pencil, or my pupil pen,
> Neither in inward worth nor outward fair,
> Can make you live yourself in eyes of men.

The suggestiveness of "lines of life" appears in the variety of commentator's paraphrases recorded in the Variorum edition: the "lines of life" can be the lines life etches on a face, or the lines of descent in a genealogy, or the lines of the living pictures presented by children, or the lines of children as living poems (as opposed to the mere written lines of the "pupil pen"), or even perhaps, as an echo at the back of the mind, what one commentator defends in urging unconvincingly that "lines of life" is a misprint for "loins of life" (compare the sonnet's conclusion: "And you must live, drawn by your own sweet skill"). Shakespeare had a supremely wandering mind! To ravel out such associations can of course be misleading. In an actual, live reading of a sonnet such clustering ideas as these are felt together, not sorted; they are the opening out of mind and heart into the plurality of the world's riches. What keeps us from coming to a standstill in walleyed contemplation is the flow of the poem's movement as it gathers in meaning in the service of the poet's love.

One can instance even more dramatic places where the poetry makes a thick harmony out of woolgathering multiplicity—the most famous is "Bare ruin'd choirs, where late the sweet birds sang," thanks to William Empson's discussion at the outset of his *Seven Types of Ambiguity*. What criticism now needs to stress, I think, is not the interplay of imagery but the interplay of sound. (A case in point is the chord of vowels and of "r's" in "bare ruin'd choirs," sounded in three successive long, slow syllables—the mystery of the line comes from this music as much as from the wonderful complex of metaphors it holds in solution.) We need to consider, not a special case like Sonnet 73, but the much more common case where there is great richness of metaphor but metaphorical consistency is not regarded:

> O how shall summer's honey breath hold out,
> Against the wrackful siege of battering days,

> When rocks impregnable are not so stout,
> Nor gates of steel so strong but Time decays?
>
> (Sonnet 65)

These are splendid lines—but it is the design of sound that chiefly carries them, the open-breathing *o* and *u* sounds and flowing consonants of "how shall summer's honey breath hold out" followed by the battering lines, with "wrackful" and "rocks impregnable." One can understand summer's honey metaphorically as provision for a siege—but one cannot carry the metaphor further, one cannot "batter" honey! And the summer-winter opposition, as well as the battering, have been lost by the time we get to "Time decays."

Sound and rhythm again and again give life to statements or figures which might otherwise be banal: so in a quatrain from Sonnet 97 selected almost at random:

> How like a winter hath my absence been
> From thee, the pleasure of the fleeting year!
> What freezings have I felt, what dark days seen,
> What old December's bareness every where!

A rich use of various *e* sounds emerges: the poignant sense of absence from "thee" is developed as we encounter the same sound in "fleeting" and "freezings"; the open *a* sounds in "What dark days" feel cavernous against the prevailing *e* tones; "December's bareness" includes the three vowel sounds present in "every where," so that the bareness seems to spread out "every where"—and the meter makes "every where" larger than it would be in prose by stressing two of its three syllables. Consonants of course are also put to work reinforcing the meaning, for example by linking "*fl*eeting and *fr*eezing" to "*f*elt," "o*ld*" to "*D*ecem*b*er," "Decem*b*er" to "*b*areness." One can go on and on in this fashion, once one starts looking for such tangible patterns—and though it is not always possible to know where to draw the line between cases that really matter and cases that are farfetched, such texture of physical relations among words is clearly fundamental to the beauty *and* the meaning of the poetry. When we shift from quatrain to quatrain, turning to lean into a new evolution, part of the newness is often the sound of a fresh set of dominant vowels; or again, we sometimes recognize a set of sounds carried all through a sonnet to give it its distinctive tune.

The Sonnets often would be "witty" if it were not that the wit in them goes along with sound and cadences that hold feeling—the wit is rarely isolated to be felt separately, as Donne's so often is, but enters into the whole motion. If we read them in isolation, we would be amused by the virtuoso alliteration and assonance in lines like

> And with old woes new wail my dear time's waste.
> . . . .
> And heavily from woe to woe tell o'er
> The sad account of fore-bemoaned moan.
>
> (Sonnet 30)

But when we read them as an integral part of the lovely sonnet "When to the sessions of sweet silent thought," the huddled sounds serve to convey the pressure of the past on the present as a thickening or troubling of speech. Where we feel a twinge of amusement, it is usually in combination with feelings dictated by the underlying rhythm, as with the ruefulness of

> But ah, thought kills me that I am not thought.
>
> (Sonnet 44)

It would be wrong to suppose that the Sonnets are without humor. There are places where Shakespeare positively romps, but the fun is almost never unmixed with serious feeling:

> Let not my love be call'd idolatry,
> Nor my beloved as an idol show,
> Since all alike my songs and praises be
> To one, of one, still such, and ever so.
> Kind is my love to-day, to-morrow kind,
> Still constant in a wondrous excellence;
> Therefore my verse to constancy confin'd,
> One thing expressing, leaves out difference.
> Fair, kind, and true, is all my argument,
> Fair, kind, and true, varying to other words.
>
> (Sonnet 105)

This gay whirl is an extreme example of the repetition common in the Sonnets, the same words rolled round, each time with added life because they fall differently each time within the poem's progress. In Sonnet 105 this sort of fun is indulged in almost by itself, in celebration of a moment's carefree confidence. But even 105, which is as near to a *jeu d'esprit* as we come, has its serious side, for it raises a question about idolatry which it does not settle.

III. "Two Loves I Have"

The publisher who pirated the Sonnets in 1640 changed the pronouns in Sonnets 15 to 126 so as to make the poems seem to be addressed to a woman; he was the first of many editors and commentators who have been troubled by the fact that a man is addressed in these love poems. Whether there was only one young man, or several, cannot be definitely settled: what is clear is that there was one role, of beloved younger friend or "lover," corresponding to a need in the poet to live in and through another person. It is usually in the beauty of a person of the opposite sex that we experience, incarnate, the sum of life's powers and perfections. But here we find that the twenty-five sonnets addressed to a woman, "the dark lady," dwell on her imperfections and falsehoods and the paradox that nevertheless she inspires physical desire; in the poems addressed to a man, by contrast, there is exultant contemplation of the beloved's beauty and cherishing of his whole identity, but nothing of specific bodily prurience. The "higher" love is expressed toward a man and the "lower" toward a woman. Poems to both, moreover, deal with a strange and troubling situation: Shakespeare's friend is lured into an affair by Shakespeare's mistress (Sonnets 40–42, 133, 134, 144); the poet's concern, in the midst of anguished humiliation, is to keep the man's love, not the woman's!

Various explanations have been offered. It has been suggested that the friend and mistress are fictions created in the process of an exercise in conventional sonneteering, but this notion has not stood up. A fiction, especially a fiction by Shakespeare, would satisfy our curiosity where the Sonnets frequently baffle us by speaking of things which the person addressed is assumed to know but to which we have no key. And much of what is expressed concerning the friend and the mistress is most definitely *not* conventional sonneteering. The claim that passionate sonnets addressed to men were conventional, with which Sir Sidney Lee and others attempted to allay Victorian anxieties, is simply not true.

It is true that there was a cult of friendship in the Renaissance, and that writers often set ideal friendship between men above love for a woman. Professor Edward Hubler, whose valuable book *The Sense of Shakespeare's Sonnets* judiciously explores this and other problems, points out that Elizabethans used the term "lover" between men without embarrassment: thus Menenius, trying to get through to see Coriolanus in the Volscian camp, does not hesitate to say to a guard, "I tell thee, fellow, Thy general was my lover." Mr. Hubler, with others, makes the further point that homosexuality, except for a passing slur about Thersites, is never at issue in the plays, either as a trait of character or, what is more revealing, as a latent motif in the imagery (Marlowe's plays provide a striking contrast). We do get in Shakespeare's comedies a series of places where boy actors play the parts of girls disguised as men; but this playful transvestism, convenient in a theater where boys played the women, is never queasy. We are never shown a man pretending to be a woman. What is dramatized is the fun of young women, Portia, Rosalind, Viola, zestfully acting as youths for a while and then falling back gladly and gracefully into their womanliness. This game reflects, not perversity, but the fundamental Elizabethan security about the roles of the sexes. The same security permitted Shakespeare to present the Duke in *Twelfth Night* delighting in the page Cesario's fresh youth and graceful responsiveness, and so falling in love without knowing it with the woman beneath the page's disguise. The sensibility of Shakespeare's age was open to appreciating qualities which youths and women have in common. This openness probably goes with the fact that homosexuality had no place in Elizabethan social life. Because their masculinity never was in doubt, men could wear their hair long, dress in silks and ruffles, pose for portraits "leaning against a tree among roses."

These facts should be kept in mind in reading Sonnet 20, where Shakespeare praises "the master mistress of my passion" for possessing feminine beauty without feminine fickleness. The bawdy joke at the end acknowledges that the friend's sexuality is masculine and directed to women; such a pleasantry could only be pleasant where physical relations of the poet with the friend were out of the question. And yet the fact remains that the relationship expressed is a most unusual one: "Mine be thy love, and thy love's use their [women's] treasure." What Shakespeare's metaphor of capital and interest here proposes is that he should enjoy the whole identity of the friend while women enjoy what this capital yields of specific sexuality. And such is indeed the sort of relationship which the sonnets to the friend express, while those to the mistress present an obverse relationship concerned with the use of her sexuality rather than with her love.

Why then do we read the Sonnets if the affections they express are so unusual? In the first place, because the love expressed for the friend *is* love, a most important kind of love which is ordinarily part of a relationship but here becomes the whole and is expressed with an unparalleled fullness and intensity. It is love by *identification* rather than sexual possession. Such cherishing love is a leading part of full sexual love between men and women. And it is central in other relations of life, notably between parents and children: the early sonnet (3) which says "thou art thy mother's glass," is followed by one where the poet is in the mother's place:

> My glass shall not persuade me I am old,
> So long as youth and thou are of one date.
>
> (Sonnet 22)

In another place (Sonnet 37) he compares himself to a father who "takes delight / To see his active child do deeds of youth." The strangely special theme of the first seventeen sonnets ("What man," C. S. Lewis asks, "ever really cared whether another man got married or not?") gives Shakespeare occasion to cherish the friend's identity and, beyond that, to envisage generously, in the idea of having children, a process by which one identity is re-created in another, as the poet throughout the Sonnets finds himself renewed in his friend.

The universality of the part of love which here becomes the whole makes it easy for us to "join," as congregation, in all those sonnets, among them the most familiar and most beautiful, where the poet expresses how the friend's being galvanizes his whole consciousness. A lover's experience is the same, whoever the beloved, when absence makes a winter (Sonnet 97), when "thy sweet love remember'd such wealth brings" (Sonnet 29), when "descriptions of the fairest wights" in "the chronicle of wasted time" seem all to be prophecies of a present beauty (Sonnet 106). These poems make one very conscious of the active transmutation of experience by passion (e.g. Sonnet 114), and of the lover's imagination straining at the limitations of physical existence: "If the dull substance of my flesh were thought" (Sonnet 44).

Loving by identifying with the person loved can have a special scope for Shakespeare which it does not have for people who are not poets, because he can realize his friend's beauty and value in words. To realize the relationship by turning it into poetry gives a fulfillment which actually is physical, in that the poem, as utterance, is a physical act. That the writing of a sonnet provides a kind of physical union with the friend explains at least in part, I think, the recurrent emphasis on the sonnets as rescuing the beloved from death. Taken literally, the talk of conferring immortality seems rather empty—the friend, after all, is never named, and he is given no determinate social identity, indeed no personality. (It is because all this area is left so blank that the curious have been free to bemuse themselves with conjectures of every kind about the friend's identity.) But the sustaining reality in the theme of immortality is that the poet, in the act of writing the poem, experiences a lover's sense of triumphing over time by becoming one with great creating nature as embodied in another being. We have dwelt on the comparison made in Sonnet 16 between different kinds of "lines of life." When the poet turns from urging children on his friend to addressing him directly, he uses the same metaphor to say that Death shall not "brag thou wander'st in his shade, / When in eternal lines to time thou grow'st" (Sonnet 18).

Such claims for poetry's power are of course a universal commonplace of the Petrarchan tradition—Shakespeare regularly links them with poignant, inclusive reflections on mortality. In reflections on mortality in carpe diem poems like Marvell's "Coy Mistress," there is often a suggestion, verging on a kind of metaphysical cruelty, that dissolution will come anyway, so it may as well come, delightfully, in sexual surrender. Shakespeare's Sonnets often enhance the beauty of his friend and the mystery of life in him by reflections that he "amongst the wastes of time must go" (Sonnet 12), like "the wide world and all her fading sweets" (Sonnet 19). The sense of helplessness in the face of time is more profound and poignant than in most love poetry, partly because Shakespeare looks to no sexual resolution. A great weight is thrown on resolution in the creative act of poetry—and so on poetry's promise of immortality. Not infrequently, as in Sonnet 19, claims made in a concluding couplet, after large reflections on devouring Time, have not weight enough to make a satisfying balance. But a massive poem like Sonnet 55,

> Not marble, nor the gilded monuments
> Of princes, shall outlive this powerful rhyme

makes us realize anew art's power of survival; in Sonnet 74 and elsewhere we are made to feel how a man's spirit can be preserved in poetry, whereas "the earth can have but earth."

IV. EROS TYRRANOS

The concern to realize and live in the identity of another is just

what we should expect, if we think about it, from the man who,
beyond all other men, created other identities. And the difficulties
with love expressed in the Sonnets are also congruous with the ca-
pacities demonstrated in the plays. One difficulty, which grows more
and more obvious as one reads and rereads the poems to the friend,
is that the action, in such a love as this, is almost all on the poet's
side. In Sonnet 53, Shakespeare asks the arresting question,

> What is your substance, whereof are you made,
> That millions of strange shadows on you tend?

The poet's powers as a dramatist at once come to mind when he goes
on to say

> Describe Adonis, and the counterfeit
> Is poorly imitated after you;
> On Helen's cheek all art of beauty set,
> And you in Grecian tires are painted new.

It is clear that the strange shadows come not from the friend, but
from the poet, who costumes him now in one role, now in another.
Sonnet 61 recognizes this fact in answering another arresting
question,

> Is it thy will thy image should keep open
> My heavy eyelids to the weary night?

The conclusion is a troubled recognition that it is the poet's will, not
the friend's:

> For thee watch I, whilst thou dost wake elsewhere,
> From me far off, with others all too near.

One is tempted to answer for the friend that after all, not being a
poet, he cannot beguile the long night with a companion composed
of images and words!

There are sonnets which recognize, too, if only playfully, that
such identification as the poet feels with his friend involves selfishness or self-love. Thus Sonnet 62 exploits a double take as to who is
who: "Sin of self-love possesseth all mine eye, / . . . Methinks no
face so gracious is as mine, / No shape so true, no truth of such
account." The turn comes with the third quatrain: "But when my
glass shows me myself indeed, / Beated and chopp'd with tann'd

antiquity." The same game is played in Sonnet 39, this time with "worth" and "self": "What can mine own praise to mine own self bring? / And what is't but mine own when I praise thee?" It is easy to dismiss this sort of reasoning, when we read a sonnet in isolation, as sonneteer's logic. But when we come to understand the sort of relationship Shakespeare is expressing, we realize that these poems mean what they say in making equations. The poet's sense of himself hinges on the identification: elation in realizing himself in the friend's self is matched by desolation when he is left in the lurch of selflessness. There are a number of poems where he proposes to do anything, to set himself utterly at naught or injure himself, if by so doing he can contribute to the friend's wishes and give him meaning: "Upon thy side against myself I'll fight, . . . / That thou, in losing me, shall win much glory" (Sonnet 88). "Speak of my lameness, and I straight will halt" (Sonnet 89). Commentators have been silly enough to conclude from this that Shakespeare was literally lame; they have argued from "beated and chopp'd with tann'd antiquity" that he wrote the sonnets when he was old. Of course in both cases what is conveyed is not literal incapacity but the poet's sense that without the younger friend he is nothing. Indeed the action of making himself nothing is, for him, a way of making love real by making the beloved everything.

With the woman, things go just the other way: Shakespeare makes love to her by telling her she is naught! At the best, he tells her that she attracts him even though she is "black" instead of "fair" (Sonnet 127); more commonly, he asks for favors in the same breath that he tells her he loves her in spite of his five wits and his five senses (Sonnet 141); most commonly, he spells out her falsehood and exclaims at the paradox that "in the very refuse of [her] deeds" she somehow makes him love her more "the more I hear and see just cause of hate" (Sonnet 150). These are outrageous poems: one wonders whether in fact most of them can have been sent to the poor woman—whether many of them were not offstage exercises in hate and despite written from a need to get something out of the poet's system. To tell a woman that since she is promiscuous, she may as well let you put in among the rest, especially since your *name* too is Will (Sonnet 135), does not seem a very likely way to win even a hardened profligate. Several poems, notably 151, present a sequence in which degrading the woman and his relation to her frees the poet for an impudent phallic self-assertion:

> For thou betraying me, I do betray
> My nobler part to my gross body's treason;
> My soul doth tell my body that he may
> Triumph in love; flesh stays no farther reason.

One cannot avoid the conclusion that, for Shakespeare, in the constellation of relations with which the Sonnets are concerned, specific sexual love was disassociated from cherishing and adoring love: Sonnet 144 summarizes these "two loves," one of "comfort," the other of "despair," one "a man right fair," the other "a woman colou'rd ill." The psychological implications have of course been variously interpreted, most recently by a Dutch psychoanalyst, Dr. Conrad V. Emde Boas. I understand that his large book, which has not yet been translated, sees in Shakespeare's cherishing of a younger man an identification with the mother's role, and a displaced narcissism which in praising the beloved enjoys the contemplation of an ideal image of the poet himself. Such a theory can only be rightly evaluated by mobilizing the whole system of thought which gives its concepts meaning. But common sense can see, I think, that the Sonnets reflect only one patterning of a kaleidoscopic personality: the tenderness which here is attached to a man or several men might well, in other phases of Shakespeare's life, have been felt for women.

And without resort to psychoanalytic formulations, our knowledge of Shakespeare's qualities as an artist can help in understanding the attitudes expressed in the Sonnets. James Joyce, in pursuing his own obsession with the artist as a natural cuckold, was much preoccupied with the triangle in the Sonnets. In *Ulysses,* Shakespeare emerges as a shadowy double for Bloom and as an omen for Stephen Dedalus: the flickering suggestions about Shakespeare center in the notion that he was betrayed because as an artist he would rather see than do, not asserting himself in actual life but taking the lead in love from others, while fulfilling himself in creating the various persons of his plays. Joyce is riding his own concerns, but he provides a useful perspective on the sonnets which deal with the double infidelity. In Sonnets 40–42, where Shakespeare struggles to find a way of resolving in words the injury that his friend and mistress have done him in deeds, the idea of his identification with his friend is carried to a bitter reductio ad absurdum:

> But here's the joy, my friend and I are one;
> Sweet flattery, then she loves but me alone.
> (Sonnet 42)

These tortured and tortuous sonnets adopt and abandon one strained interpretation after another, including the ironic suggestion that the two others are behaving as they do only to satisfy Shakespeare vicariously:

> Loving offenders, thus I will excuse ye,
> Thou dost love her, because thou know'st I love her,
> And for my sake even so doth she abuse me,
> Suff'ring my friend for my sake to approve her.
>
> (Sonnet 42)

How much simpler it would be if friend and mistress were both of them in a play! Indeed, bitter as these sonnets are, they express a response to the humiliation life has brought which moves in the direction of art. Most men would bury the event in silence, or else turn injury into anger. Shakespeare turns injury into poetry. The very act of writing about the betrayal is a kind of acceptance of it—which goes with the extraordinary effort to accept the friend even in such circumstances. Thus Sonnet 41 excuses "Those pretty wrongs that liberty commits, / When I am sometime absent from thy heart," only to exclaim poignantly, "Ay me, but yet thou might'st my seat forbear." In Sonnet 40 the poet attempts a gesture of total self-abnegation:

> I do forgive thy robb'ry, gentle thief,
> Although thou steal thee all my poverty;
> And yet love knows it is a greater grief
> To bear love's wrong than hate's known injury.
>   Lascivious grace, in whom all ill well shows,
>   Kill me with spites; yet we must not be foes.

The whole metrical force of the sonnet is mobilized in the uttering of "Lascivious grace," a phrase which brings into focus the anguish and enjoyment of Shakespeare's continuing identification with the friend. The poet's artistic sympathy encounters the ruthlessness of another living identity and remains open to it.

These are disturbing and unsatisfying poems, despite their great power, because they do not achieve a stable attitude toward the experience. We encounter the same irresolute quality in some of the sonnets where the young man's dissoluteness or vanity are both rebuked and accepted (e.g., Sonnets 95, 84). The poems are twisted on the rack of a sympathy "beyond good and evil," the sympathy which is organized in the plays, flowing into opposites and antagonists so that, as Eglington phrases it in *Ulysses,* "He is the ghost and the prince. He is all in all." Stephen Dedalus takes up the point:

> He is, Stephen said. The boy of act one is the mature man of act five. All in all. In *Cymbeline,* in *Othello* he is bawd and cuckold. He acts and is acted on. . . . His unremitting intellect is the hornmad Iago ceaselessly willing that the moor in him shall suffer.

These are wild and whirling words, describing Shakespeare through Stephen and his preoccupations. But in them Joyce brings out how much Shakespeare needed the drama.

V. Self-knowledge

The most satisfying of the sonnets which deal with Shakespeare's difficulties in love are those where he is using the sonnet primarily to confront what love reveals to him about himself. Thus in Sonnet 35 we get, in the midst of excuses for the friend, a recognition that

> All men make faults, and even I in this,
> Authorizing thy trespass with compare,
> Myself corrupting, salving thy amiss.

The most impressive explorations come in sonnets which are late in the numerical order—poems which have a complexity of texture and tone which set them apart from most, though not all, of the first one hundred, and so were probably composed later. Among those to the woman, I find most satisfying the ones which, forbearing hymns of hate, define the cheapness of the relation—cheapness being one of the hardest things to get into poetry (or indeed to face up to in any fashion). Symmetrical lies are laid out in Sonnet 138, hers to him and his to her, tea for two and two for tea:

> Therefore I lie with her, and she with me,
> And in our faults by lies we flattered be.

A stimulating criticism by Mr. Patrick Cruttwell, which relates these late poems to the plays of the period of *Hamlet* and *Troilus and Cressida,* sees this sonnet as "perhaps the most terrible of the whole sequence," climaxed in the "grim seriousness" of the pun on lie. "Grim" seems to me wrong: I find the poem jaunty as well as devastating, and more honest so. Where the sonnets to the woman do become completely grim, there is usually a certain falsifying simplification in resorting to unmeasured abuse, as in the couplet which ends, but does not resolve, the analysis of love's fever in Sonnet 147:

> For I have sworn thee fair, and thought thee bright,
> Who art as black as hell, as dark as night.

In the poems of self-analysis addressed to a man, there is a far deeper facing up to the poet's own moral involvement—and to the paradoxes of passion where morality seems no longer to apply. In Sonnets 109–112 and 117–121 the poet, acknowledging infidelities on his side, confronts directly the polymorphic responsiveness of his own personality:

> Alas 'tis true, I have gone here and there,
> And made myself a motley to the view,
> Gor'd mine own thoughts, sold cheap what is most dear,
> Made old offences of affections new.
>
> (Sonnet 110)

Here "made myself a motley" suggests the actor's impulse and his humiliations, and in Sonnet 111 Shakespeare explicitly asks his friends to forgive in him the "public manners" which are bred by the "public means" from which he must provide for his livelihood:

> Thence comes it that my name receives a brand,
> And almost thence my nature is subdu'd
> To what it works in, like the dyer's hand.

Commentators have emphasized, indeed exaggerated, the ignominious status of the acting profession in the Elizabethan age, seeing in this outward circumstance the source of Shakespeare's self-disabling humility toward his friend. No doubt it was a factor, just as part of the appeal of the young man or young men was superior birth, a heritage the poet did not have and could enjoy through identification. But the temperament which made Shakespeare an actor and dramatist is more fundamental than the matter of status, as these sonnets make clear: they present a complex, resonant personality which, for most purposes in life, is overresponsive, overeager, drawn on to act unworthy parts and unable to avoid living out in new relationships what has already been found shameful. His fluidity, his almost unbearable openness to desire and to life, are described in Sonnet 109 in the course of a moving plea:

> Never believe, though in my nature reign'd
> All frailties that besiege all kinds of blood,
> That it could so preposterously be stain'd
> To leave for nothing all thy sum of good.

The sort of knowledge of the heart and its turnings which finds expression in the plays appears in these sonnets with a special if limited intensity—the intensity involved in seeing, in one's single life, the broken lines made by Eros. In the same moment when he asks forgiveness for making "old offences of affections new," Shakespeare has the courage to recognize that there is value, as well as humiliation, in selling "cheap what is most dear":

> Most true it is, that I have look'd on truth
> Askance and strangely. But by all above,
> These blenches gave my heart another youth,
> And worse essays prov'd thee my best of love.
>
> (Sonnet 110)

There is no set posture in these poems against morality or convention: if they simplified things by adopting a romantic or bohemian rationale, they could not be so serious in exploring the way passion turns corners that it cannot see around and moves in directions contrary to the will. Sonnet 121 confronts in a frightening way the breakdown of moral categories in this territory: " 'Tis better to be vile than vile esteemed. . . . No, I am that I am." The pressure of experience on received categories is so great in this sonnet (and at places in others of this whole group), that it is impossible entirely to comprehend the meaning—though we can apprehend it obliquely. In the dramatic form, Shakespeare could present directly, in several persons, what here is looked at askance from one vantage.

These poems reckoning with himself are not the greatest sonnets Shakespeare wrote, though they are profound and moving. The poems which gather in life with a lover's delight have more sensuous substance than these inward-turning pieces; and the poems which generalize out from love have more that each reader can make his own. There is not space to consider some of the most wonderful of the generalizing sonnets, such as the tough yet poignant evaluations of worldliness, Sonnets 124 and 125 ("Pitiful thrivers, in the gazing spent?"), the analysis of lust as "Th' expense of spirit in a waste of shame" in Sonnet 129, the large-souled gesture of fidelity in Sonnet 116, "Let me not to the marriage of true minds / Admit impediments," or the urgent religious revulsion from life in Sonnet 146, "Poor soul, the centre of my sinful earth." These great poems, because they generalize, can be appreciated in isolation. The sonnets confronting his own nature, by contrast, grow in meaning as we set one against another—and as we see the whole group in relation to what Shakespeare did in his plays. Few poems have expressed so close to the heart and nerves as Sonnet 120 the transformation of suffering into compassion:

> That you were once unkind befriends me now,
> And for that sorrow which I then did feel
> Needs must I under my transgression bow,
> Unless my nerves were brass or hammer'd steel.
> For if you were by my unkindness shaken,
> As I by yours, y'have pass'd a hell of time,
>
> . . . .
> O that our night of woe might have remember'd
> My deepest sense, how hard true sorrow hits.

Here we see particularly clearly how the capacity for identifying with a person loved, sometimes disabling, perplexing and humiliating, also gives Shakespeare his "deepest sense, how hard true sorrow hits."

Criticism and the Analysis of Craft: The Sonnets

Rosalie L. Colie

By the Sonnets we are also invited to become critics, urged to experience something about the writing of poetry, the making of fictions, and the meanings of poetry to a poet and to any literate man. Where *Love's Labour's Lost* played with the literary stock conventions and devices, imposed a literary-critical skepticism upon the play's plot, action, and characterization, the Sonnets do something else, dramatize literary criticism. Where *Love's Labor's Lost* emptied so many conventions of their conventional freight, the Sonnets animate, among other significant and characteristic conventions of the genre, the self-referential, self-critical tendency in sonneteering itself.

Critics of Shakespeare's sonnets consistently remark on the dramatic quality of the sequence (or sequences, or series, or cycle, or cycles: the exact relation of the poems to one another is difficult to establish); and compared with other great Renaissance sonnet-sequences, English and Continental, the marked quality of Shakespeare's sonnets is, certainly, that dramatization into personality of Renaissance sonnet personae and conventions. Whatever the order of composition or the poet's "intent," the arrangement of the poems (by the author? by the editor? by the printer? by chance?) manifests someone's awareness (for simplicity's sake I assume that someone to have been the poet) of a loose but nonetheless involved and involving "plot." The arrangement of the characters into two triangles—poet-friend-mistress; poet-friend-rival poet—is, so far as I know, unpar-

From *Shakespeare's Living Art.* ©1974 by Princeton University Press.

alleled in Renaissance sonneteering, although there are adumbrations of both relationships in sonnet literature. Two friends' love for the same lady is by no means unknown in romance and comedy; literary theory and practice sanctions sonnet-commentary on stylistic subjects. Shakespeare's sonnets work with the conventions of the literary genre in a remarkable way, possibly most boldly in this triangulation of personalities, by which the poet turns tradition upside down and inside out to examine the "real" implications of conventional utterance and, in some cases, to force these implications to new limits in the situation, poetical as well as psychological, which is the poems' donnée. What other Renaissance poet praises his cult-friend in terms normally reserved for the sonnet-mistress *and* devotes considerable sonnet-time to a mistress as well—a mistress who is herself notably atypical in the genre? Further, though many sonneteers qualify conventional admiration of ladies by denouncing their particular ladies for one or another real or fancied fault of love, what sonneteer settles down to love his lady, knowing that she has played him false and doubtless will do so again? Merely in the development of his psychological story, Shakespeare has managed to make important statements about the relation of a literary love-code to specific experiences of loving. As in his other works which deal with love, Shakespeare investigates that difficult, involving, threatening, fulfilling experience, examines both its *mores*—its customs and its morality—and its rhetoric, or, to stretch definitions for rhetoric, the poet examines the relation of its expressive style to behavior.

What are the psychological situations of love which can or should be expressed in lyric poetry, and what are valid ways of speaking about these problems? How does a poet deeply committed to his craft manage to honor the traditional conditions of love-literature *and* to express the particularities of a man's emotional response to his particular experience of love? In the Sonnets, many kinds of disappointment are examined: disappointment in a continuing relation to a cult-friend; disappointment in a mistress; disappointment by these two in concerted preoccupation with one another, shutting the poet out of both relationships; disappointment with the self as lover and as poet; even, at times, disappointment with poetry itself. That is not the only mood, of course; it is, though, a mood at variance with the traditional attitudes of love-poets writing sonnets—and the persuasiveness of this poet's disappointment is in part a result of the rarity of that mood in sonnets.

Certainly the sonnet-lover conventionally presented himself as constantly analyzing and revising his psychological condition, but Shakespeare manages to treat the human relationships postulated in his sonnets so problematically, to make such "real" problems of them, that a standard self-analytic pose has been considerably enriched and deepened. For instance, when love for a friend conflicts with love for a mistress, what happens to the lover of both? Another way of saying this, pointing more exactly to the literary problem, is: How does a writer handle these two versions of idealized love, faced off against one another? What decorum suits such a conflict, and in what persona ought the poet to speak? Unlike *Love's Labor's Lost,* where he tackled the "mereness" of the love-conventions, in the Sonnets, Shakespeare set himself to realize—that is, to provide body and mind for—the psychological and literary problems raised by love and the literary love-plot, problems to which he returned again and again through his productive life.

In his sonnets Shakespeare experiments with materials repeatedly used in the sonnet-genre and alters these materials so that his series, though perfectly traditional in shape and in topic, almost leaps from the official limitations altogether. As one reads through, for instance, the English sequences gathered in Sir Sidney Lee's collection, one is first struck by the fact that this genre itself seems to be an invitation to repetitiousness—or, if one prefers the term, to *copia;* and not from poet to poet merely, but within a single poet's work as well. The genre itself requires acceptance of a theme and that theme's variations. Second, one cannot help noting how deviant Shakespeare's sonnets are, not in their repetitiousness, but from the *norms* of repetitiousness—even when, as he does, he asks a young man to marry in seventeen different sonnets!—how peculiarly personal the poems are, within a genre in which conventions of self-expression, self-analysis, and self-reference are extremely highly developed. Some of this independence on Shakespeare's part may be "merely" historical, a factor of the decade in which he came to sonneteering, as Patrick Cruttwell's perceptive essay [*The Shakespearean Moment*] suggests. No doubt Shakespeare was favored by the generation into which he was born, but so is any gifted poet, as we see after the fact. Shakespeare took advantage of his advantages; not only as inheritor but as legator too of poetic and dramatic practice, he was partly responsible for changes in modes of expression in English writing at the turn of the century. Shakespeare's talent was such that it could not be buried in the earth, or hid under a bushel: in the Sonnets, as in his dramatic experiments, he tackled difficult problems, penetrated deeply into the traditions he was using, with the result that those traditions were themselves permanently altered by his having submitted himself to them.

However deviant Shakespeare's sonnets seem when set against contemporary practice, nonetheless they are just as profoundly rooted within the sonnet-tradition. Dante set the mode for a concerted sequence in which repeated quatorzains were a major element; and once Petrarch had written his extraordinary sequence, inevitably the extended lyric narrative, made up of short poems, became one of the great Renaissance forms, a "modern" invention apparently owing little to antiquity. By giving his verses a surround of prose commentary which filled in narrative gaps, commented on his own poetic efforts and intentions, and examined his own lyric feelings in greater detail than the short poetic form then permitted, Dante built into the sonnet-sequence its tendency to *literary* as well as private, personal, and lyric self-criticism; the same scrutiny was directed at the poet and the poetry he was writing, a tendency which left its mark on the whole sonnet-tradition. The sonnet was by no means the only lyric form to comment on itself: several medieval forms, especially the *canzone,* permitted and encouraged comment by the poet on his own verse and his aspirations for it, and poetical self-reference occurs in many classical forms (lyric, epigram, ode). In sonnet-sequences, anyway, such self-commentary was accepted as a subtheme, until there were sonnets on sonnets, sonnets on the sonnet-form, long before Wordsworth or John Updike produced their sonnets–on–sonnets.

The literary-critical sections of the *Vita Nuova* are in prose, not poetry: the verses lie, separate jewels, in display cases of prose which serve several different purposes, only one of which was Dante's self-explication. Petrarch wrote his sonnet-commentary into his sonnets themselves; Lorenzo de' Medici prefaced his with a prose disquisition, the *Comento;* in Bruno's *Gli eroici furori,* at the end of the long tradition, the sonnets are set, like occasional marks of punctuation, in a sea of discursive prose, as illustrations for the topics under discussion. Petrarch's poetry, originally innocent of prose, did not lack prose commentary for long; his editors, some of them Petrarchan poets themselves (as Bembo was), provided explanation, explication, critical commentary, and justification for Petrarch's lines. Many *petrarchisti* made their reputations both by their own poetry and by commenting on their master's. Lecturing on Petrarch, like lecturing on Dante, became a major critical enterprise in Florence, so that a poet like Tasso, for instance, could write significant essays on single poems by Petrarch, by Della Casa, and by himself. In imitation of such respectful treatment of Petrarch, editors sprang up for the other vernacular lyric writers of the Renaissance, of whom Muret is the most distinguished, who edited Ronsard—indeed, one mark of Ronsard's official success was the attention his verse received from humanist and fellow-poet editors, conscious of their models to the south.

Clearly, then, sonnets could and did become one major opportunity for literary self-reference and self-commentary, not only in the poet's official duty to examine his own inward self, but also in his opportunity for critical comment on his own work and on the traditions in which he was at work. Dante's prose commentary on the verses of the *Vita Nuova* offers one kind of self-concern, Petrarch's stylized, romantic self-presentation of his maturing self another. Ronsard everlastingly commented on himself and his earlier poetical achievements (even, by extension, the ladies celebrated in earlier sequences), and Du Bellay's lyric poetry records his relation to his own poetry. Ronsard quotes himself so playfully as to raise interesting questions of tone and dedication, in a genre primarily epideictic. Sidney, who was much indebted to Ronsard's example, played his own self-referential games in *Astrophel and Stella*—at the linguistic level, often self-consciously skirting the destruction of the very poems he was writing, as he denied his poetic and stylistic aims in sonnets which set out to demonstrate and to illustrate (masterfully, I think) those very aims he criticized.

Sidney's sonnets celebrate a lady, though quite differently from Petrarch's orderly, clear, sequential celebration in the *Canzoniere,* and differently too from Ronsard's ultimately sequential series of se quences, which "progress" from the childlike nymph Cassandre to the mature, high-born, well-named Hélène. But again and again, Sidney returns to consider, and sometimes to celebrate, poetry; he tests the limit of possibilities of his conventional resources, and of language itself. "What may words say, or what may words not say?" becomes one of the major preoccupations of his lyric sequence, and stands as the fundamental, eminently quotable, classically succinct question about all utterance. His debate is conducted in fairly conventional terms—of Muse, of purling spring, of Aganippe well—thoroughly relevant to sonneteering; but so is the larger question of celebration as truth or as flattery:

> What may words say, and what may words not say,
> Where truth it selfe must speake like flatterie?

The "given" of the sonneteer is the beloved's perfection: what have grammar rules, dictionary's method, or allegory's curious frame to do with such self-evident revelation as Stella's beauty?

Sidney writes directly into his verse those problems peculiar to the sonneteer's exercise; he knows his own, and his models', relation to "poore *Petrarch*'s long deceased woes," and knows too that if he manages to persuade of the uniqueness of his lady and his love, he must do so by a native, not a denisened, wit. Part of the fascination of Sidney's sequence lies in the tension between his exploitation of the tradition, with all its grandiloquence of language and allusion, and the criticism to which the tradition is so overtly subjected.

Perhaps because Sidney's sonnets so manifestly do just this, Shakespeare's sonnets do not explore that paradoxical self-contradictoriness which so punctuates Sidney's *Astrophel and Stella*. Though they have their share of the conflicting rhetorical tropes, oxymoron and paradox, Shakespeare's sonnets rarely rely on technical manipulation of grammar and rhetoric to overcome deliberately self-courted poetic self-destruction. This is not to say that Shakespeare has not his own ways of making us note his skill at sonneteering: he makes impressive variations on the subjects and themes conventional in sonnet-sequences and expected by their experienced readers. As Stephen Booth has so brilliantly demonstrated in his modestly stated and important study [*An Essay on Shakespeare's Sonnets*], Shakespeare could and did manipulate several linguistic and structural systems in his sonnets at once, balancing one off against another to achieve effects very different from those of other sonneteers. Like Sidney, Shakespeare came at the end of a long European preoccupation with the sonnet, and was therefore able to range from one to another end of the stylistic and thematic gamut appropriate to the genre, from conventional Petrarchan opposition and hyperbole, through the sweet fluency of Bembo and Ronsard, to the relative simplicity of Du Bellay's or Wyatt's vernacular styles. Here, I want to touch only on his ways in the Sonnets of commenting on poetry, his own and other poets', his ways of managing criticism within the narrative frames he constructed.

We might begin with the standard trope for poetic immortality, the *monumentum aere perennius*—"Not marble, nor the gilded monuments / Of Princes shall outlive"; "Devouring Time, blunt thou the lion's paws"; "So long as men can breathe, or eyes can see, / So long lives this, and this gives life to thee"; "Since brass, nor stone, nor earth, nor boundless sea"; "His beauty shall in these black lines be seen, / And they shall live, and he in them still green." Again and again, the poet reiterates the poet's boast that verse can distill the truth of a man's transient life to its purest essence, that verse is a vial to hold that essence forever. And the classical immortality conferred by verse lives wholly in the poet's gift; he offers or withholds— though with this generous poet, there is no question of withholding whatever he might give. This poet, as his verse records, spent his talents only to find them still green, still growing with (significantly mixed metaphor) "spending" and "use." Gradually, poetic immortality moves out from a trope of art (*monumentum*) to images of natural creativity: in Sonnet 115, for instance, the poet incorporates his growing poetic capacity and his present love in a single body— "Those lines that I before have writ do lie; / Even those that said I could not love you dearer." But since "Love is a babe," in the conventional reference to Cupid, as love grows, so does creative power, closely allied with, dependent upon, the love "which still doth grow."

The *monumentum* trope in many variations is proudly displayed in these poems proud of their subject. The poet recognizes no equivocation about the value either of friendship or of the poetry celebrating this friendship, as the verse itself becomes a monumental epitaph to the friend's perfections. Implied in the trope itself is the memorial function of verse, officially centered in the epigrammatic tradition, of which the epitaph was a part. Navarre's opening speech in *Love's Labor's Lost* notes the relation of fame, epitaph, and poetry. Here, poetry, that implying art, comes to replace the monolithic precision of incised epitaph:

> Who will believe my verse in time to come,
> If it were fill'd with your most high deserts?

Though yet, heaven knows, it is but as a tomb
Which hides your life and shows not half your parts.

(Sonnet 17)

Or I shall live your epitaph to make,
Or you survive when I in earth am rotten;

. . . .

The earth can yield me but a common grave,
When you entombed in men's eyes shall lie.
Your monument shall be my gentle verse,
Which eyes not yet created shall o'er-read;
And tongues to be your being shall rehearse,
When all the breathers of this world are dead.

(Sonnet 81)

The appeal, across the grave and across the monuments marking men's lives, to any reader—*our* eyes, then "not yet created," now o'er-read these lines, to fulfil the poet's prophecy and his boast—extends the meaning of the bookish convention to include an ongoing life; "breathers" marks life's simplest function, and at the same time reminds us of the etymology of poetic inspiration. With a poet in hand, a poet's friend can economize on marble and gilded monuments, may trust to the poet's muse, with whom it lies

To make him much outlive a gilded tomb,
And to be prais'd of ages yet to be.

(Sonnet 101)

The poet invokes, then, both the precise and cryptic quality of epitaphic praise and the grandiose boast of the lyric poet's conference of immortality upon his subjects—the poetry of statement and the poetry of praise fuse in this remarkable conflation of traditions generally quite separate.

This method of taking a metaphor literally, of forcing its implications on readers, is of a piece with Shakespeare's practice generally and is one indication of his essentially critical attitude toward his materials. Perhaps even more telling are those examinations of his work as he goes along, writing, it seems, with one eye on himself writing:

Who will believe my verse in time to come?

(Sonnet 17)

Let this sad int'rim like the ocean be.
Or call it winter,

(Sonnet 56)

Shall I compare thee to a summer's day?

(Sonnet 18)

—with its implied "no," and its given reasons why such a simile is inadequate to the subject. In Sonnet 21, the poet rejects "couplement of proud compare," to describe his love's excellence for its simple, plain truth; in Sonnet 59, he considers the whole problem of "invention":

If there be nothing new, but that which is
Hath been before, how are our brains beguil'd,
Which labouring for invention bear amiss
The second burden of a former child!

Love, inextricably joined to poetic creativity, has been a "babe," "still growing"; the poem-monument had appealed, across death, to living generations yet to come. Now, in 59, even searching for poetic language is likened to the labor-pains of a mother, disappointed in her second, counterfeit issue:

O, that record could with a backward look,
Even of five hundred courses of the sun,
Show me your image in some antique book,
Since mind at first in character was done!
That I might see what the old world could say
To this composed wonder of your frame;
Whether we are mended, or whe'er better they,
Or whether revolution be the same.
O, sure I am, the wits of former days
To subjects worse have given admiring praise.

The sonnet plays with the idea central to the *de inventoribus* trope; Shakespeare assumes as true the burden of Curtius's rediscovery for us, that classically-influenced literature (to say nothing of human habits of thinking) was marked by a series of formulae, schemes, *topoi*, by which a man was relieved of the responsibility for "invention" required of poets since the romantic revolution. The poem also looks toward the possibility of cyclic return, less a cultural than a natural return, by which this young man may simply be seen, wonderfully, as a later manifestation of some beauty authoritatively commented on "in some antique book." The whole question, then, is raised of a poet's relation to his profession's past, without losing sight of his ever-present responsibility for *epideixis,* the praise of a specific "you," an identifiable subject. Although the poet sounds as if his own invention were exhausted and suggests also that, all invention being merely repetition, either of words (*topoi*) or of a reincarnated beautiful object, he welcomes a literary situation in which he is required to parrot ancient phrases and tropes, he nonetheless belongs to the self-consciously modern era, and must bring into question that authoritative ancient achievement. "Whether we are mended, or whe'er better they, / Or whether revolution [i.e., cosmic time-changes] be the same" may repeat some ancient notions about historical events, but it calls into question the conviction that the ancients had a monopoly on correctness. The couplet has a weary ring, as if the poet, knowing the bad habits of poets in his day too easily persuaded to mere sycophancy, could not trust his dead colleagues, those unquestioned ancient masters, to have been more accurate than contemporary poets in praising their subjects.

The poet who called his friend "the tenth Muse, ten times more in worth / Than those old nine which rhymers invocate" (Sonnet 38), and who so identified his verse with his love and himself with his friend that he could write "O, how thy worth with manners may I sing, / When thou art all the better part of me?" (Sonnet 39), recognized that actual "breath"—his friend's presence, conversation, and company—was the inspiration of his poetry. Not of his "invention" merely, which could work even in the friend's absence (Sonnets 27, 98), but of his creativity—Sonnet 27 records how the image of the friend blots out all others, and 98, a "Zefiro torna" with a difference, how

> Yet nor the lays of birds, nor the sweet smell
> Of different flowers in odour and in hue,
> Could make me any summer's story tell,
>
> . . . .
>
> Nor did I wonder at the lily's white,
> Nor praise the deep vermilion in the rose:
> They were but sweet, but figures of delight,
> Drawn after you, you pattern of all those.

Sonnet 113, on the other hand, demonstrates the poet's metaphorical powers at work: whatever he sees, in his friend's absence, he converts into the image of his friend:

> The mountain or the sea, the day or night,
> The crow or dove, it shapes them to your feature;

and, in Sonnet 114, he can "make of monsters and things indigest / Such cherubins as your sweet self resemble." In these poems, we see the image-making process at work, watch the poet watching his own figuring forth in verse, his impossible matching of all things, good and bad, crow and dove and monster, to his obsession.

This record, however, runs counter to the constant stress on poetic "truth"—the friend is the poetry's ornament, which thus needs no ornament drawn from the manuals of rhetoric and poetics. "Couplement of proud compare" is rejected for "the sweet ornament which truth doth give." A poet with such a subject has no need for art, no need for figure, no need for invention, since the subject itself, simply named, confers sufficient perfection upon verse.

In this connection, the slander-sonnets are interesting, in that they recognize in the slanderers' fictions a kinship with the poet's problems of expression. First of all, the very perfection which, by its signaling in verse, confers upon that verse a special value causes slander in real life, "the ornament of beauty is suspect," by its mere existence. But at the same time, there may be some truth in the slanderers' comments (Sonnet 69), since his detractors judge the friend by his behavior—in the conventional overstatement of slander, as in the conventional overstatement of poetry, there is some matching of this particular, specific young man's qualities. Withal, in the end, the poet must charge the friend's enemies with fiction, though, as with the overstatements of his own poetry, he must count, even in its apparent dispraise, their fiction as a kind of praise:

> That tongue that tells the story of thy days,
> Making lascivious comments on thy sport,
> Cannot dispraise but in a kind of praise:
> Naming thy name blesses an ill report.
>
> (Sonnet 95)

When his own reputation was at stake, however, the poet did not find things so easily resolved: "ill report" running about him was not so quickly turned to the service of fictive praise. On the contrary, that ill report sent him back, as proper sonneteer, to face himself as he was in naked self-examination, to assess himself and the slander about him. " 'Tis better to be vile than vile esteemed" is a line unthinkable about the friend; but he makes it, with its elaborate defense, about his own condition:

> When not to be receives reproach of being,
> And the just pleasure lost, which is so deemed
> Not by our feeling, but by others' seeing.
>
> (Sonnet 121)

As in the poems to his mistress, in which the poet's reproaches turn into an opportunity for self-assessment apparently detached, here too others' disapproval, however painful, offers a chance to make his own critique of himself, far closer to the facts of the matter than any outside criticism:

> For why should others' false adulterate eyes
> Give salutation to my sportive blood?
> Or on my frailties why are frailer spies,
> Which in their wills count bad what I think good?

This sonnet is remarkable for its prosiness: "When not to be receives reproach of being" is exact and euphonious, but entirely without imaginative, figurative imagery. Quite different from the effort in the poems to the friend, the language here strives toward bareness and simplicity of statement, as in the remarkable turning:

> No; I am that I am; and they that level
> At my abuses reckon up their own.

Nothing could be plainer, and nothing more daring, than this paraphrase of the Almighty's self-declaration in an unadorned poetic language which, precisely for that reason, commands belief.

The poet's plainness of statement becomes a poetic position, polemically defended in the Rival Poet series. Once upon a time he could say, fearing no particular threat, that he wrote of his friend "without all ornament"; once upon a time, could imagine his friend favoring his poems, after his death, even though they were mere "poor rude lines" compared with "the bett'ring of the time." Then the friend might be imagined as saying,

> "But since he died, and poets better prove,
> Theirs for their style I'll read, his for his love."
>
> (Sonnet 32)

But when an "alien pen" has actually attracted the attention and favor of this friend, then the poet must reconsider his whole relation to poetry, and to poetry specifically as persuasion, as a means to the beloved's grace. Unquestionably, his style is not high—he is "a worthless boat," a "saucy bark" compared to the vessel "of tall building and of goodly pride" now riding on the "soundless deep" of the friend's patronage (Sonnet 80). Now his own "gracious numbers are decay'd," his Muse is sick: he must "grant, sweet love, thy lovely argument / Deserves the travail of a worthier pen" (Sonnet 79); but, like himself and all the poets instructed by and in their connection with his friend, this new poet can do no more than repeat, as he so long has done, the subject's beauty. The question of matching comes up in another context: "I never saw that you did painting need," he says, plaintively,

> I found, or thought I found, you did exceed
> The barren tender of a poet's debt;
>
> (Sonnet 83)

> Who is it that says most which can say more
> Than this rich praise—that you alone are you?
>
> (Sonnet 84)

Because of the plainness of his style, then, his critical friend, recognizing how short the celebration has fallen of his true worth, must "seek anew / Some fresher stamp of the time-bettering days." But rhetoric alone, the verbal instrument designed for persuasion, cannot persuade:

> yet when they have devis'd
> What strained touches rhetoric can lend,
> Thou truly fair wert truly sympathiz'd
> In true plain words by thy true-telling friend.
>
> (Sonnet 82)

Finally, because of the misery of the separation and the misery of his own inadequate inspiration, he can only be tongue-tied, dumb, and mute (Sonnets 83, 85), trusting in silence an eloquence more persuasive than "the proud full sail of his great verse" (Sonnet 86).

Sonnet 76 shows an enlarged perception into the psychology and also the sociology of poetry:

> Why is my verse so barren of new pride?
> So far from variation or quick change?
> Why, with the time, do I not glance aside
> To new-found methods and to compounds strange?

In these lines, there is the recognition that, in literary fashions, novelty counts, and that his own verse is not, in this sense, fashionable. The next quatrain moves from the general situation, in which time is taken to confer a "bettering" upon poetry, to his personal situation within the craft:

> Why write I still all one, ever the same,
> And keep invention in a noted weed—

to his own style of "clothing" his thoughts:

> That every word doth almost tell my name,
> Showing their birth, and where they did proceed?

Here, style as fashion comes into the sharpest conflict with style as individual expression—and, we gather from the plot constructed around the problem, which has provided "reason" for examining the problem in the first place, individual style must go down before the time's dictation. But, by the compliment's familiar turning, the poem's logic defends the poet's tautological reiteration of the friend's perfections, justifies the poet's practice altogether:

> O, know, sweet love, I always write of you,
> And you and love are still my argument;
> So all my best is dressing old words new,
> Spending again what is already spent;
>   For as the sun is daily new and old,
>   So is my love still telling what is told.

In the triumphant, and entirely conventional, figure of the sun's faithful return after its nightly extinction, bringing light and fertility to the world each day, the poet establishes the essential nature both of his love, and of his way of expressing that love. Human expression must triumph over fashion, and even over art.

The Rival Poet sonnets form one of several groups of separation-poems, in which the poet sings, studies, and comes to terms with his estrangement from his friend. Certainly he has been "absent" from the friend in earlier sonnets, and he has incurred the friend's displeasure too. But *this* separation is cast entirely in poetic terms: not only is the poet's love called into question, but so is the language he uses, his professional personality. Restoration of the friend's favor brings poetic reunion (Sonnets 97–103) as well, and the Muse is roused to celebrate the refound love—"return, forgetful Muse"; "Rise, resty Muse"; "O truant Muse"; "Make answer, Muse"; "Then do thy office, Muse"—which is, to reassert the values of the poet's poetic convictions:

> "Truth needs no colour with his colour fix'd;
> Beauty no pencil, beauty's truth to lay;
> But best is best, if never intermix'd."
>
> (Sonnet 101)

The repetitiousness, the familiarity of the poet's style is, finally, justified by a perverse application of the doctrine of imitation: "Fair, kind, and true" must be his only argument because those are the intrinsic qualities of the young man praised. Fashion is rejected, finally, for the truth of plain speaking:

> What's in the brain that ink may character
> Which hath not figur'd to thee my true spirit?
> What's new to speak, what new to register,
> That may express my love or thy dear merit?
> Nothing, sweet boy; but yet, like prayers divine,
> I must each day say o'er the very same;
> Counting no old thing old, thou mine, I thine,
> Even as when first I hallowed thy fair name.
>
> (Sonnet 108)

Sonnets 108 to 113 reconsider the separation now happily ended: the poet examines himself, in some of the sharpest analytical sonnets he ever wrote. In "Alas, 'tis true I have gone here and there / And made myself a motley to the view," the poet gives himself no quarter, save in the assertion that "worse essays prov'd thee my best of love." Fortune has not favored him, by committing him to a life which forces him to deviation from his best self:

> O, for my sake do you with Fortune chide,
> The guilty goddess of my harmful deeds,

> That did not better for my life provide
> Than public means which public manners breeds.
> Thence comes it that my name receives a brand.
>
> (Sonnet 111)

In a marvelous image, full of self-disgust and yet speaking through that disesteem to his own professional commitment to his art, the poet comments on the "public means" which so threaten him:

> And almost thence my nature is subdu'd
> To what it works in, like the dyer's hand.

"Like the dyer's hand"!—stained by the dyes, marked by its service to the materials of its art, that hand can nonetheless make new patterns, must prepare cloth to useful and decorative functions, as the poet, his whole being steeped unmistakably like the dyer's hand in the materials of his own craft, shapes new patterns for new poetic purposes, chooses the colors (of rhetoric and of poetics) to make social ends beautiful. The poet's verse, to which he is servant, speaks to other people and will do so "Till all the breathers of this world are dead."

Clearly, the relation of poet to this friend is based on poetry: poetry is not only the conventional instrument of appeal to patron, friend, and lover, the conventional voice in beauty's praise; but poetry is also the poet himself, ingrained in his personality and thus marking (the dyer's hand) all his human realizations and relations. That Shakespeare has provided poetic theory with a body and a personality in the fictive Rival Poet, around whom he organized a drama of verse and about verse, thereby invigorating an entirely academic convention of sonnet metapoiesis, is less surprising than that he thereby intensifies and dramatizes recurrent questions of styles— of praise, of imitation, of self-projection. The Rival Poet is invoked not as a voice for "style" of verse simply, though he unquestionably is made into a topic for discussing that subject. Because in this poet's prodigal economy, verse so clearly *is* the man, and a chosen style so interpenetrated with its poet's personality, the Rival Poet becomes an animate, breathing threat to our poet's continued life as poet, as friend, as man, a threat which can only be warded off by a purified rededication to poetic integrity. What Shakespeare's whole creative effort demonstrates is, I think, that for him poetic integrity lay in the continual reexamination of poetic values, the continual confrontation of those problems literature always sets for poets. In *Love's Labor's Lost,* the mereness of style is endlessly and lovingly exposed as the fraud that it is, the miracle of creation reduced to an examination of craft—and the value of skill in the service of literary creativity reaffirmed even as its illusionism is exposed. From the Sonnets, we learn something else: how a man's fundamental moral existence can be a matter of style.

Commentaries on the Sonnets

Stephen Booth

SONNET 116

Sonnet 116 is the most universally admired of Shakespeare's Sonnets. Its virtues, however, are more than usually susceptible to dehydration in critical comment. The more one thinks about this grand, noble, absolute, convincing, and moving gesture, the less there seems to be to it. One could demonstrate that it is just so much bombast, but, having done so, one would have only to reread the poem to be again moved by it and convinced of its greatness.

A major problem about literary art is that abstract general assertions do not feel any truer than their readers already believe them to be; they carry no evidence of their truth and very little of the life (and thus very little of the undeniability) of the physically extant particulars from which they derive. Descriptions of those particulars, or exempla, or metaphoric allusions can bring life and conviction to a generalization, but they also limit its range and its value to the reader. The attraction of abstract generalizations is the capacity they offer us to be *certain o'er incertainty* (115 11), to fix on a truth that allows for and cannot be modified by further consideration of experience or change in our angle of vision. One means of achieving universality and vividness at once is bombast: high-sounding, energetic nonsense that addresses its topic but does not indicate what is being said about it, and thus rises free of human intellectual limita-

From *Shakespeare's Sonnets*. ©1977 by Yale University. Yale University Press, 1977.

tions like a hot-air balloon. Bombast, however, is rarely satisfying for long or to any listener who pays attention to the signification of the words he hears strung together. Bombast overcomes the difficulties of language by abandoning its purpose; a general, noble, vibrant utterance that conveys no meaning operates like a bureaucracy that functions perfectly so long as it ignores the purpose for which it was established.

Sonnet 116 has simple clear content; indeed, its first clause aside, it is one of the few Shakespeare Sonnets that can be paraphrased without brutality. That alone excludes it from classification as bombast, but much of its strength and value is of the same sort that bombast has. Sonnet 116 achieves effective definition unlimited by any sense of effective limitation. One obvious source of that success is that its positiveness is achieved in negative assertions (a definition by negatives is minimally restrictive because the thing so defined may be thought to possess all qualities but those specifically denied). Some of the means by which negative definition is made efficient, convincing, and satisfying in this sonnet are those that can be used to give grandeur to nonsense.

The sonnet combines extreme generality—even vagueness— with locutions that imply some degree of personification and thus invest abstract statements with the urgency, vividness, and apprehensibility of concrete particulars. That occurs in obvious fashion in the straightforward navigation metaphors of quatrain 2, but the equation of *love* with a seamark or a star only *explains* the speaker's meaning, is a chosen substitute for the speaker's topic, a substitute that acknowledges by the necessity of its use that the actual topic remains a distant impalpable essence, sensorily apprehensible by imperfect proxy. Other, less openly supportive effects do more toward achieving the special grandeur of this poem than the navigation metaphors. Consider the effects of *the remover, looks,* and *bears it out;* each operates differently, but they have a common denominator in giving effective concreteness to the identity of ideal love, in at the same time reasserting that that essence is indeed disembodied and incapable of comprehension in images, and in insisting that what is here encompassed and made apprehensible is nonetheless too big, too grand, too spiritual to be grasped. In line 4, *the remover* presents an embodied characteristic left free of any specific body or kind of body; it suggests all—but specifies none—of "people who are inconstant," "time (which is the remover of beauty, the alterer)" and "a departed lover (one who has ceased to requite the love given him, or one who has literally gone to another place, or one who is dead)." The shadowy personification of *the remover* lets us do something like visualize an actor and action without knowing at all what they are.

Similarly, *bears it out* in line 12 means only "persists," "endures," but suggests positive particular action, allowing a reader to visualize action, motion, and power, without visualizing any actor, mover, or wielder of power; *it* suggests specific objectivity, but has no antecedents and therefore no more particularity than in the modern phrase "stick it out," meaning "endure." *Bears it out* suggests an heroic striding forth, but no visualizable strider; it is not limited or diminished, and not being ostentatiously figurative, does not advertise its identity as a mere translation of the unknowable into knowable terms.

Lines 5–7 present another instance of abstract statement that has the vividness of sensually perceived action. The assertion that love *is an ever-fixèd mark* is simple metaphor; it explains. The statement that a seamark *looks on* is another matter. The sense is clear enough; the focus of concern dictated by *ever-fixèd* makes *looks on* an effective synonym for "endures," "persists in the face of." That a seamark should be said to "look" also makes sense (as does the same action by a *star* in line 7); the most effective seamark is a beacon (see *OED* examples from 1566 and 1617); a Renaissance reader would recognize the aptness of the image both from the way a beacon looks at night and because Shakespeare's contemporaries were used to speaking of eyes as if they emitted the light they reflect and see by (see 20.6). The statement that a seamark *looks on tempests and is never shaken* is also apt; a tiny distant flame that withstands the wind and water of a tempest is as fitting an emblem of steadfastness as the ever-fixed North Star in the next line. None of that is poetically remarkable. What is remarkable is that the logic in which *looks on* indicates "persists," the logic in which a seamark is eye-like and can be considered capable of looking, and the logic in which a feeble but constant flame is emblematic of steadfastness are independent of one another; each supports the assertion without reference to its relation to the other two. As a result the statement gets all the validity of the seamark's concreteness but remains mystic and wonderful, made as resistant to comprehension as available to it—and by the same locution. Moreover, whatever else it does, *looks on* personifies the insensate seamark as a beholder, although the function of seamarks is exactly opposite. On the other hand, the beholders, the sensate mariners who are guided by seamarks and stars, are presented (by metonymy) as *every wand'ring bark,* i.e., as boats.

None of that is at all complicated until it is explained. The lines do not demand any explanation; they are immediately clear, but they derive much of their power from being both simple and straightforward and simultaneously so complexly wondrous that beholder and beheld are indistinguishable from one another in a statement that makes their ordinary relationship perfectly clear.

A similar blend of substantial and insubstantial fabric occurs on a larger scale in *Love is not love* (line 2) and in *I never writ, nor no man ever loved* (line 14). In those two cases the speaker's meaning is clear and immediate, uncolored by the incidental supernaturalness inherent in metaphoric perception; at the same time, both assert absolute nonsense. *Love is not love* is a traditional (and traditionally pleasing) kind of incidental paradox in which a straightforward assertion (in this case "That kind of love is not genuine love") is phrased so as to be meaningless if taken literally. Similarly, the hyperbole of the couplet is so extreme that it merely vouches for the speaker's intensity of feeling; it gives no evidence to support the validity of his statement because on a literal level it is ridiculous (we cannot doubt that what we read was written). Moreover, though the special meaning "truly loved" is obvious in *no man ever loved,* that assertion, like *Love is not love,* gets its rhetorical power from the ostentatious falsehood of its unmodified literal sense.

The discussion of Shakespeare's devices for simultaneously emphasizing particularity and vagueness, substance and emptiness, brings us to a related technique in Sonnet 116 that has related effects: the poem is both single-minded, presenting constancy as the only matter worth considering, and heterogeneous in ways that do nothing to diminish or intrude upon its single-mindedness. In examining the special appeal of Sonnet 116, it may be well to remember that in saying anything—no matter how general—one advertises the fact that one has *not* said everything else—everything else pertinent to one's topic and everything else impertinent to one's topic. That may sound less simpleminded and more worth saying if one considers the related proposition that the literary creations we value most are works like *Hamlet, King Lear, Paradise Lost,* and *Ulysses,* works so full—so full of matter, so full of different kinds of matter, and so open to being viewed from so many angles of vision—that their particulars seem to include all particulars, and the experience of them seems to take in all experience and all attitudes toward it. Sonnet 116 is overlaid with relationships established in patterning factors that do not pertain to or impinge upon the logic and syntax of the particular authoritative statement it makes. The most obvious of them, of course, are the formal iambic pentameter rhythmic pattern and the sonnet rhyme scheme. This sonnet, however, also contains patterns of a kind that falls between the ideational structure (what the poem says) and the substantively irrelevant phonetic patterns of the sonnet form: patterns established by the relationship of the meanings of its words—in this case meanings that are irrelevant to, and do not color, the particular sentences in which they appear here but which do pertain generally to the topic about which the sentences isolate particular truths in particular frames of reference.

Let in line 1 and Admit in line 2 both have the general sense "allow," but Let can mean "stop," "prevent," "impede" (as in Hamlet 1.4.85: "I'll make a ghost of him that lets me" and in this marginal gloss to the Geneva text of Psalms 115: "No impediments can let his worke, but he useth even the impediments to serve his wil" [gloss (c); Shakespeare echoed gloss (f), which says that the makers of idols are "As muche without sense, as blockes & stones," in Julius Caesar 1.1.36; he echoes the Psalm itself in 137.2]). Similarly, "to admit," meaning "to allow to enter," and impediments, as things that prevent entrance, also have an extra-syntactic relationship. (Also note O no in line 5; the exclamation not only contains the sound of the casually auxiliary imperative "O know [that]" but also presents a logically incidental example of a suitable prefatory exclamation introducing an impediment volunteered by a parishioner responding to the injunction in the marriage service that "if any man can show any cause, why they may not lawfully be joined together, let him now speak.")

The meanings of true in line 1 are "faithful" ("constant to one another") and "steadfast" ("constant in intent," "unwavering"), but, since marriage of true minds has overtones of the Christian and Platonic ideal of purely spiritual love, of true minds can also suggest "which is truly of minds (or souls) rather than merely of bodies"; true meaning "not a lie" pertains generally to truth-telling, the topic of this sentence, even though that sense of true is not evoked by the syntax or admissible in it; true meaning "straight," "not bent," implies the rightness, the spiritual health, of constant minds and is balanced by the idea of "becoming bent" inherent in bends in line 4.

Bends, which is used to mean "turns aside," "changes its direc-

tion," contains untapped potential for nearly contrary meanings irrelevant to its use in line 4 but relevant to the general topic of constancy: "to bend to" means "to apply all one's energy, attention, and
concern on one object"; the "to bend to" construction here adds the
idea of fixed intent on removing to the contrary idea of turning aside
(see *bent to . . . cross* in 90.2 and *bent / To follow* in 143.6–7); *bends*
also suggests stooping (as opposed to the staunch uprightness of the
seamark in the following line) and submission (as opposed to the
steadfastness required to withstand time's *bending sickle* in line 10—a
line in which *bending* echoes *bends* but describes the curving blade of
a sickle, the curving stroke with which a sickle is wielded, the bending of the grass before it, and the submission of grass to blade). In
line 11, *alters* echoes *alters* and *alteration* in line 3 where they follow
immediately upon a precise echo of a church service performed at an
altar (see 115.6 and 116.1–2).

In line 10, the reference of *his* is specified by *sickle* (because Father Time has traditional association with a sickle, and the other
available antecedents do not). In line 11, the same reference for *his* is
dictated by the model of the previous *his,* by the obvious substantive
link between *time* and *hours and weeks,* and—most importantly—by
the context of the poem's general argument that love is permanent.
However, the line includes—and thus acknowledges within the
poem's triumphant sweep—the altogether arguable proposition
which the whole poem denies, the proposition that love is fleeting,
the proposition which *Love alters not with his brief hours and weeks*
would imply if those words stood alone as a paradox in which the
syntactic norm prevailed, *Love* were the antecedent for *his,* and the
line presented this paradox: "Love, with its brief hours and weeks
(love, which is characterized by its brevity), alters not." As read in
context the line says, "Love alters not with *time's* brief hours and
weeks," and that straightforward and single-minded sense is absolute—is absolutely undiminished, is absolutely unmodified, and is,
in fact, absolutely strengthened by the self-contradiction engulfed
within it.

Compass means "encircling reach" and "sphere of influence" in
line 10, but appears in context of a quatrain-long metaphor of navigation to which "mariner's compass" pertains.

One sense of *error* in line 13 is a synonym for one sense of
wand'ring in line 7. As one comes upon the word, *error* suggests "that
which is erroneous," "not true," and thus recurs to the specific con-

cern of the portion of the marriage service echoed in lines 1 and 2: telling the truth; *upon me proved* is an obvious legal metaphor, and its juxtaposition with *error* narrows the meaning of that word to "heresy," "a false creed," and makes the whole line a specific metaphoric allusion to formal accusations of false belief (see Sonnet 105) and inconstancy in religion. The completed line, however, still refers back to the marriage service echo but takes another ideational route to get there: the passage echoed in lines 1 and 2 comes from the general section of the service where the congregation is asked to present evidence that the marriage cannot morally or legally go forward. The idea of doomsday (introduced by *to the edge of doom* in line 12) is also abstrusely relevant to matrimonial impediments; the priest asks the bride and groom if they know any impediment why they may not be lawfully joined together and charges them to answer as they "will answer at the dreadful day of judgment."

That tangle of incidental relationships surely never enters into a reader's understanding of the lines; presumably it never touches his consciousness even to the extent that rhythm, rhyme, and alliteration do; every habit of purposefully used and purposefully comprehended language leads a reader to ignore the ideational static in what he hears. In this sonnet, however, the denseness of incidental meaning patterns and their close ideational relevance to what the speaker is saying are sufficient to make the poem's assertions sound as if they took cognizance of all viewpoints on all things related to love and were derived from and informative about every aspect of love.

The best example of effective expansion of the scope of a narrowly based generalization is the undercurrent of frivolous sexual suggestiveness in the poem. High-principled definitions of true love are ordinarily inefficient because they exclude not only sexuality but the human habit of taking the topic of sexuality lightly, joking about it. Many of the metaphors and ideas of this sonnet seem just on the point of veering off toward puerile joking about temporary male impotence—loss of tumescence—after sexual climax and about temporary abatement of female sexual desire; quatrain 2, for instance, is always ready to turn into a grotesquely abstruse pun on "polestar." Most of the sexually suggestive elements in the poem are obvious and in more danger of being exaggerated than missed (but see 80.7, [*bark*], 137.1, [*fool*], *mark* in *Love's Labor's Lost* 4.1.123–29, and *rose* in *As You Like It* 3.2.101–2; with reference to *looks* in line 6, see Eric Partridge, *Shakespeare's Bawdy*, s.v. "eye" and "naked seeing self").

That is not to say that Sonnet 116 is an elaborate dirty joke masquerading as a grand statement of grand principle (any more than Sonnet 115, which in technique and effect is the mirror image of this one, is a solemn philosophic statement masquerading as a toy); here one cannot find a coherent sexual undermeaning as one can in schoolboy jokes like "My dame hath a lame tame crane" or even Drayton's "Since there's no help," but the poem does offer a substratum of random bisexual references that suggest preposterous teasing based on the ridiculously logical argument that a male lover is inconstant, not faithful, untrue in love, if his sexual potency is not constant, and a female is likewise inconstant if she is temporarily sated.

Sonnet 116 is probably valued not because it asserts the value of absolute fidelity, but because it is itself so absolute, so "certain o'er incertainty," that it can both recommend and successfully demonstrate single-minded allegiance to one governing principle. The poem testifies by example that single-mindedness, authority, and certainty can exist—or seem to exist—without a fanatic narrowness of reference.

The triviality, irrelevancy, and baseness of the sexual innuendo in Sonnet 116, its indecorum, is a source of the poem's value, its success, and its grandeur. As with the incidental complexities, contradictions, and by-meanings discussed previously, the very pettiness of the sexual overtones contributes to the impression the poem gives that its general, all-inclusive, absolute, grandly simplistic moral imperative is genuinely general, that it presents a genuinely definitive definition, one that excludes no particulars or attitudes that might modify or challenge it, one that has been tested by all exceptions that might prove its rule wanting, one that is both absolute and absolutely true.

Sonnet 129

Sonnet 129 was the object of "A Study in Original Punctuation and Spelling," an exercise in irresponsible editorial restraint written by Robert Graves and Laura Riding (originally called "William Shakespeare and E. E. Cummings" in *A Survey of Modernist Poetry* [London, 1927], revised and retitled for inclusion in Graves's *The Common Asphodel* [London, 1949], from which I quote it). The essay contains some palpable gaffes (e.g., "the Elizabethans had no typographical *v*"—which appears less than two inches from "very wo") in their transcription of the Q text of 129.11 [the Elizabethans did not use *medial v*]). However, the textual sanctimony of Graves and Riding has proved infectious. The essay starts out by describing Cummings's use of typographical idiosyncrasies for communicating nuances ("Cummings protests against the upper case being allotted to 'I': he affects a humility, a denial of the idea of personal immortality responsible for 'I'. Moreover, 'i' is more casual and detached: it dissociates the author from the speaker of the poem"; they then introduce Sonnet 129 and their intent in the essay: "By showing what a great difference to the sense juggling of punctuation marks has made in the original sonnet, we shall perhaps be able to persuade the plain reader to sympathize with what seems typographical perversity in Mr. Cummings. The modernizing of the spelling is not quite so serious a matter, though we shall see that to change a word like *blouddy* to *bloody* makes a difference not only in the atmosphere of the word but in its sound as well." They quote both the Q text of Sonnet 129 and the modernized text in *The Oxford Book of English Verse* and then proceed to compare them. Since the Graves-Riding essay is still often treated with respect, I will excerpt it at length and comment on it parenthetically in support of the proposition that an editor distorts the sonnet more for a modern reader by maintaining the 1609 text than he would if he modernized its spelling and punctuation:

"First to compare the spelling. As a matter of course the *u* in *proud* and *heauen* changes to *v;* the Elizabethans had no typographical *v*." (I agree that the *u*'s in Q's "proud" and "heauen" are to be read as *v*'s, but I see no benefit in making a reader interrupt his reading to translate them; moreover, leaving "proud" in Renaissance orthography is to maintain an attractive nuisance: a modern reader does well to recognize that an ocular pun on "proud" [= modern "proved"] and "proud" [= modern "proud"] may have momentarily crossed a Renaissance reader's mind and that the context of this poem is one that makes the sexual senses of "pride" and "proud" pertinent [see 151.10]; that, however, can all be managed in a note. To offer Q's "proud" to a modern reader is to invite ingenious speculations on the possibility that Shakespeare meant us to understand "proud" as "in a state of pride" *rather than* as "proved.")

"There are other words in which the change of spelling does not seem to matter. *Expence, cruell, bayt, layd, pursut, blisse, proofe, wo—* these words taken by themselves are not necessarily affected by modernization, though much of the original atmosphere of the poem is lost by changing them in the gloss. Sheer facility in reading a poem is no gain when one tries to discover what the poem looked like to the poet who wrote it." (I am uncertain what the authors mean by "the original atmosphere"; if this is an argument for preserving quaintness, then what is preserved is obviously not original. I do not understand the logic of "when" in "when one tries to discover," but surely to see the text Shakespeare and his contemporaries saw is not to see it as they saw it. It would not look quaint or cute to them; they would have no trouble reading it. Is it not an editor's aim to make a modern reader's experience of the text as like as possible to that of the audience for which it was written? Whenever an editor modernizes a text, he risks distorting it; whenever "the plain reader" looks at an unmodernized Renaissance text, he risks distorting it; since one of them must stick his neck out, it should be the one who is trained and paid to do it. No editor is likely to succeed perfectly in accommodating a modern reader and a Renaissance text to one another, but that is no reason to do nothing.)

"But other changes designed to increase reading facility involve more than changes in spelling. *Periurd* to *perjured,* and *murdrous* to *murderous,* would have meant, to Shakespeare, the addition of another syllable." (Yes, but to a modern reader the change from "periurd" to "perjured" does *not* mean the addition of an extra syllable. "Murderous" is another matter; in modern English it is pronounced with two syllables or, more often, with three; "murd'rous" will indicate the dissyllabic pronunciation demanded by the rhythm.)

"*Inioyd,* with the same number of syllables as *periurd,* is however printed *Enjoy'd;* while *swollowed,* which must have been meant as a three-syllable word (Shakespeare used *-ed* as a separate syllable very strictly and frequently allowed himself an extra syllable in his iambic foot) is printed *swallow'd.* When we come to *despised,* we find in the modern version an accent over the last syllable. These liberties do not make the poem any easier; they only make it less accurate." (The objection to "Enjoy'd" is valid; since a modern reader customarily reads "enjoyed" as a dissyllable and since the rhythm of line 5 encourages that reading, the spelling "Enjoy'd" is a pointless gesture of editorial vigilance; however, Graves and Riding ask us to take a case against thoughtless editing as a case against all editing. The case for Q's "swollowed" is badly founded: I know of no point in any Shakespearean text where one can reliably say from the spelling of any word what pronunciation "must have been meant." The statement beginning "Shakespeare used" should begin "Thomas Thorpe's employees used" or "Shakespeare's printers used"; even so the statement is inaccurate: Shakespeare's printers did not use -*ed* so very strictly: see 26.11, 85.6, 97.8, 10, 120.4, etc. Moreover, allowing for the extra final syllables of feminine rhymes, I do not see that—in the Sonnets—"Shakespeare allowed himself an extra syllable in his iambic foot"—although, since spelling does not always indicate syncopation or show things like the fact that, as in modern British English, "flowers" is pronounced both dissyllabically and monosyllabically in Shakespeare, there are a good many apparent instances to the contrary, instances that prove to be ocular when one listens to the rhythm of the lines where they appear. One cannot be certain, but the case for dissyllabic pronunciation of "swollowed" ["swollowed" or "swol-wed"], seems at least as strong as the case against. The sentence on "despised" apparently intends to register disapproval of the editorial spelling "despisèd," which seems to me only a useful signal to the modern reader that his usual pronunciation of the word is inappropriate to the rhythm of line 5 and that the usual Elizabethan pronunciation is called for instead. The assertion that editorial "liberties" make the poem less accurate is true only if one seeks an accuracy calculated to maximize the disorientation of the modern "plain reader," to make his experience of the poem less rather than more like an Elizabethan's.)

"The sound of the poem suffers through re-spelling as well as through alterations in the rhythm made by this use of apostrophes and accents. *Blouddy* was pronounced more like *blue-dy* than *bluddy;* the *ea* of *extreame* and *dreame* sounded like the *ea* in great; and *periurd* was probably pronounced more like *peryurd* than *pergeurd*." (Graves and Riding may well be right about the Elizabethan pronunciations of "bloody"; they could be right about "extreme" and "dream"; their speculations on "perjured" are not provoked by any evidence I know of. In any event, their real problem lies in their assumptions about the usefulness of Renaissance spellings as indicators of Renaissance pronunciations. Such assumptions are foolish in considering English spelling in any period; see Holofernes on "doubt," "debt," "calf," "half," etc., in *Love's Labor's Lost* 5.1.2ff. They are particularly foolish for Elizabethan texts in which a word may be spelled in several different ways on a single page; see 118.5. No Elizabethan writer or printer could have expected his reader to recognize variations in spelling as signs of variations in pronunciation. Surely we cannot assume that Shakespeare's reader heard Q's "bloody" in 50.9 differently than "blouddy" in 129.3. Graves and Riding seem to recommend the retention of "extreame" and "dreame" as guides to the Renaissance pronunciation of those words, but, even if we knew how Shakespeare heard them, Q's "ea" would not indicate the vowel sound of "great" to a modern reader. One might re-spell all of Shakespeare to conform to educated guesses about Shakespeare's dialect; a reading that pronounces "blouddy" as "blue-dy" and "dream" as "drame" and does not also readjust all the other words in the poem will turn out only an affected hybrid. Having chosen a dialect—say that of a Warwickshire boy who has spent some years in London—and having guessed at its sounds, one might then reproduce it casually, i.e., follow the method indicated by Graves and Riding in "blue-dy," which would signal one pair of vowel sounds in London, another in Chicago, and several others in the several parts of South Carolina; one might instead transcribe one's guesses into phonetic symbols, thus making Shakespeare legible only to a few specialists who could make their own transcriptions and who would probably reject one's guesswork in favor of their own. All in all, a modernized text—one that indicates rhythmic necessities with apostrophes and accent marks and uses occasional speculative notes where rhyme, rhythm, or wordplay call a change urgently to our notice—is probably the least unsatisfactory of the unsatisfactory possibilities open to us.)

Graves and Riding give the bulk of their essay to comparing and interpreting the punctuations of the Q text of 129 and the modernized text in *The Oxford Book*. They make two general points, one negative and valid, the other positive and invalid. Their whole discussion is an implicit argument against inflicting logically directive modern punctuation on lines in which a word or phrase participates in more than one syntactical structure, and in which the experience of a modern reader leads him to take punctuation marks as signals of logical limitation—as indicating which of the several relationships in which a word or phrase participates is the "right" one. Any student of the Sonnets has probably at some time been dismayed by one or another instance of wanton clarification and wishes that editors would not feel obliged—and that the usual implications of punctuation did not oblige them—to authenticate one syntax in a passage and muffle the others. That discomfort with edited texts probably prompted the Graves-Riding essay and probably also accounts for the respect the essay has commanded. There are a good many points in the collection where two syntactical structures overlap (or, in the phrase of Graves and Riding, interpenetrate one another), and where a modern reader may feel the need of some clarifying and diminishing punctuation, and where most modern editors have provided it (see, for example, 89.7). Unfortunately for the practical value of the Graves-Riding essay, Sonnet 129 is neither diminished nor altered by modern punctuation. . . . In 129 modern punctuation gains "sheer facility in reading" and denies a modern reader nothing that Shakespeare's contemporaries would have perceived. The modern punctuation does lessen the probability that a modern reader will attempt to read the Q punctuation as a Cummings-like clue to meaning. In fact, as their justifications for retaining the Q text of 129 develop, Graves and Riding illustrate the dangers inherent in their misplaced textual fidelity by themselves demonstrating the wanton ingenuity that can result when a modern reader brings twentieth-century expectations about spelling and punctuation to an early-seventeenth-century text.

In the midst of their increasingly tortured revelations about Sonnet 129, Graves and Riding offer the following persuasive platitude: "Shakespeare did not write in the syntax of prose but in a sensitive poetic flow." Be that as it may, readers read in the syntax of prose. If they did not, some of Shakespeare's and all of E. E. Cummings's poetic devices would fail. Graves and Riding come to grief because they ignore the power of syntactic genre to direct a reader's expectations. For example, they argue that the comma usually inserted after "bloody" in line 3 distorts the Q text, "Is periurd, murdrous, blouddy full of blame,": "A comma after *blouddy* makes this a separate characterization and thus reduces the weight of the whole phrase as rhythmic relief to the string of adjectives; it probably had the adverbial form of *blouddily.*" I am not sure what the authors mean by "had the adverbial form *blouddily,*" but, if they mean to suggest that Shakespeare could have expected his contemporaries to understand "bloodily" when they read "blouddy," they are wrong. Even if there were any evidence of "bloody" ever being used adverbially in the Renaissance, the family likeness between the ordinary adjectival sense of "bloody" and that of "murd'rous" and "full of blame" will lead—and always would have led—any reader to take line 3 as "Is" plus a sequence of four separate but equal adjectival units. A

Renaissance reader, brought up on haphazard printing and casually rhetorical punctuation, must necessarily have been particularly sensitive to syntactic signals and more likely to understand "bloody" as a third entity in the sequence "perjured, murd'rous, bloody" than modern editors or readers are. All the retention of Q's "blouddy full of blame" achieves is the need for a cautionary note reminding the reader that "bloody" does not occur as a British slang substitute for "very" until the eighteenth century.

Much the same sort of counterargument may be made to the defense of Q's "and very wo" in line 11. One could, and Graves and Riding do, squeeze a meaning out of the phrase; it is not impossible that Shakespeare actually wrote "and" and not "a"; but it is highly improbable that a seventeenth-century reader would have done other than modern editors do: "a very woe" makes ready sense in context; "and very woe" does not. Shakespeare would have been uncharacteristically foolish to have used the Q phrase, which (unlike the non-communicative elements in 112.7–8, 14 and 113.14), has no apparent witty allure, and which he would surely have expected his reader to emend in passing. E. E. Cummings could assume an audience prematurely and permanently scarred by spelling bees and lessons in punctuation; he could communicate by deviating from the norms. An Elizabethan reader knew no such norms. Moreover, he was used to correcting printer's errors as he read—much as we do now when we read the haphazardly proofread "early bird" editions of daily newspapers; even we do not infer editorial comment when we see a story datelined "Loss, Angeles."

Graves and Riding also overestimate the power punctuation has on modern readers. In line 2 *The Oxford Book* text substitutes a semicolon for Q's comma after "lust in action"; Graves and Riding complain that the change results in "a longer rest than Shakespeare [or the printer] gave; it also cuts the idea short of *action* instead of keeping *in action* and *till action* together as well as the two *lust's*." That makes good sense in terms of handbooks on punctuation, but I do not think one reads the line differently with a semicolon in it than with a comma. Graves and Riding also object because "a comma is omitted where Shakespeare [*sic*] was careful [*sic*] to put one, after *bayt*. With the comma, *On purpose layd*—though it refers to *bayt*—also looks back to the original idea of *lust;* without the comma it merely continues the figure of *bayt*." "On purpose laid" has double reference whether there is or is not a comma after "bait"; the line-end pause insures that. Even for modern readers, punctuation does not govern the logic of a sentence except in rare cases where syntax and general context do not dictate the logic. Mistakes in punctuation are usually obvious; if punctuation had the powers Graves and Riding assume for it, would we not misread all the sentences in which we note mispunctuation or in which we simply overlook misplaced commas and missing question marks.

Graves and Riding conclude their essay by citing Quince's prologue to "Piramus and Thisby" (*A Midsummer Night's Dream* 5.1.108ff.: "If we offend, it is with our good will. / That you should think, we come not to offend, / But with good will."). The speech prompts Quince's audience of courtiers to make jokes about his bad punctuation. Graves and Riding take the passage as evidence for their thesis. Note, however, that the opening lines of Quince's prologue would have the same immediate effect if the period after "our good will" and the commas after "think" and "offend" were removed:

> If we offend, it is with our good will
> That you should think we come not to offend
> But with good will.

The line-end pause after "our good will," the effect that the resultant reading of the first line has on "That you should think," and the ellipsis between "think" and "we," all operate to an effect that the punctuation merely confirms. If Quince, a writer with a poor ear for syntactic signals, had had another and more talented actor to speak his prologue, the actor would have seen the misdirections in which the syntax leads and compensated with careful phrasing (e.g., by hurrying across the stop at the end of the first line and stressing "But" in the third). If Quince's prologue were not obviously an intentional burlesque, an editor might repunctuate the lines in an inevitably unsuccessful attempt to make them say what Quince ought to be saying in a gracious prologue. Editors do in fact do that with many passages in the Sonnets that use gentler versions of the techniques Shakespeare used in making Quince ridiculous; the editors usually fail and have to write notes claiming success. Such editors are the targets for Graves and Riding, but Graves and Riding disable themselves by joining their adversaries in overestimating the power of punctuation and the efficacy of logic over syntactic habit, and in underestimating the power of idiom to lead a reader where he expects it to lead him. Shakespeare's Sonnets are full of sentences in which the speaker is like Quince in that the signals inherent in his situation and the signals inherent in his syntax, diction, and idiom are at cross purposes. Editors and critics should avoid trying to strengthen some signals and diminish others, but they do no one a service if they augment Shakespeare's plentiful supply of linguistic crises by fabricating them in poems like Sonnet 129.

Sonnet 146

I have elsewhere examined several critical accounts of Sonnet 94 in an effort to demonstrate the illogic and folly of habitually thinking about a Shakespeare sonnet in terms of "either . . . or" and "is . . . but" and to recommend thinking in terms of "both . . . and" and "is . . . and is also" (*An Essay on Shakespeare's Sonnets*). Sonnet 146 is a subtler poem than 94 and the experience of reading it is less jarring intellectually, but both place their readers' minds so as to look at facts from a single point of view (thus inviting critics to demonstrate the exclusive pertinence of that point of view), and also lead them inevitably to look at the same facts from other and incompatible points of view (thus inviting critics to deny that their minds wander from the frame of reference the poet demands or to deny that the overt intent and effect of the sonnet are what they seem to be). Sonnet 146 has recently prompted two valuable essays—B.C. Southam's, which takes issue with the critical consensus on the sonnet, and Charles Huttar's, which takes issue with Southam. The essays are valuable in themselves and valuable as demonstrations that this sonnet (like most of Shakespeare's Sonnets) is satisfying to read, unsatisfying to think about, and likely to evoke critical analyses that satisfy only by *making* the poem satisfying to think about. These two essays are more open-minded, more responsible, and more sensible than essays in the controversy over Sonnet 94 have been, but in a sophisticated form they too exhibit the debilitating effects of insisting that anything that is true must be exclusively true and that the presence of one implication necessarily diminishes the force of counter implications that are also present.

One of my purposes in writing the present commentary on the Sonnets is to advertise a criticism that does not try to say how a work should be read or should have been read in the past but instead concerns itself with how the work *is* read, how it probably *was* read, and why. The following cavilling comments on the Southam and Huttar essays are intended as witness to the wisdom and practical necessity of a criticism that admits that every impression that a poem evokes in the majority of its modern readers and can be demonstrated as a probable response in the majority of the poet's contemporaries is and was a part of that poem and cannot be argued away. I hope that the following discussion will also explain how the glosses I provide throughout this commentary are to be used and why I gloss in the pluralistically-committed way I do.

I will start with Huttar's efforts to gloss a single phrase, *these rebel pow'rs* in line 2. He successfully argues that the phrase refers to nonphysical faculties, to the passions, the affections, the emotions, the lower powers of the soul. He quotes John Wylkinson's 1547 translation of Aristotle's *Ethics* in probably unnecessary support of his point:

> The Solle of Man hath thre powers, one is called the lyfe vegitable: in the whiche man is partener with trees & with plantes: The second power, is the life sensible in the whiche a man is partener with beastes, for why al beastes haue lifes sensible. The third, is called solle reasonable, by the whiche a man differeth from all other thinges, for there is none reasonable but man. And this power reasonable is sometyme in acte, and sometime in power, from whence the Beatitude is whan it is in acte and not when it is in power.

However, Huttar does not succeed in his argument that Southam and the world at large are "wrong to take 'these rebbell powres' as referring to 'the physical being.'"

Huttar stresses the distinction between the flesh and desires of the flesh. Huttar assumes not only that making the distinction is valid, which it is, but that the distinction bears on this poem, which it does not. He offers Donne's Holy Sonnet 14 ("Batter my heart"), *Faerie Queene* 2.11.1–2, and other examples of the Renaissance commonplace by which "the relation of reason to the other powers" of the soul is presented in images of war—particularly civil war—between reason and the passions and in images of reason besieged by the affections; he harnesses them thus:

> The affections are part of the soul; yet they besiege "the fort of reason" in order "to bring the soule into captiuitie."

Here is precedent for Shakespeare's addressing himself to the whole soul in line one, then referring to only a part, reason, by the "thee" of line two. The role of the body is to augment the onslaught of affections through the infirmity of the flesh; but if the servant is obedient to the master . . . *both body and soul are saved together.*

The insistence of the Christian creeds on the resurrection of the body clearly shows that the concept of the body as a prison, which the soul is better off rid of, is rejected. . . . In Christian thought the body is not to be done away with but to be redeemed (Rom.viii:23) by being changed (Phil.iii:21; I Cor.xv:20,35–54). . . . The body is not inherently evil but potentially good or evil, as Romans vi:12–19 makes clear.

I think that a major source of the misunderstanding is the ambiguity of the terms "flesh" and "body" in the New Testament. The Epistle prescribed by the *Book of Common Prayer* for the third Sunday after Easter admonished Christians to "abstain from fleshly lusts, which war against the soul." St. Paul testifies, "I know that in me (that is, in my flesh,) dwelleth no good thing" (Rom.vii:18), and "I keep under my body, and bring it into subjection" (I Cor.ix:27). Flesh and spirit are clearly opposites (Rom.viii:5–13; Gal.v:16ff.). Christians are to "mortify the deeds of the body" (Rom.viii:13, part of the Epistle for the eighth Sunday after Trinity). It is easy to see how such passages could be read Platonically.

In fact it is hard to see how they could be read otherwise; Pauline and Platonic thinking were intertwined from the beginning and became more so with the passage of time. The best evidence of their fusion is the long history of efforts by philosophers and theologians to disentangle them; no one works at disentangling what is not entangled. Huttar cites, quotes, and joins the disentanglers: "The Reformers resisted" the idea that the body is necessarily evil:

Calvin commented on Romans vii:18: "Both these names therefore, as wel of the flesh as the spirit agree vnto that which reteyneth stil his naturall affection." "Flesh" then in Scripture was taken as symbolic of the "rebbell powres" of the soul, the affections. This metaphorical sense is ob-

vious in Galatians v:24, "They that are Christ's have crucified the flesh with the affections and lusts." To read "have
crucified the flesh" literally is absurd. But unless we are
on guard we shall read "flesh" and "body" literally and
thereby risk the error of calling biblical that which is really
neo-Platonic. We shall be in danger of forgetting that extreme asceticism actually is frowned upon in the Bible
(e.g. Col. ii:23; I Tim.iv:4).

The danger Huttar fears is surely genuine; the reformers' urge to
avert it, the traditional readings of the sonnet, Huttar's urge to deny
them, and the sonnet itself all testify to that. However, it is doubtful
that the word "danger"—meaning something that *can* be averted,
something that is not inevitable, and something that *should* be
averted—is appropriate to discussing this sonnet; the elements that
evoke the responses Huttar finds theologically inappropriate are ingrained in the sonnet, and a discussion that excludes them as "mistaken" can have validity only in an essentially biographical argument
that Shakespeare wanted to write a poem other than the one we have
and failed to see that he had not written it. Such an argument would
be hard to sustain but would be a legitimate enterprise; such an argument would not, however, be about this poem but about something else. Huttar's logic finally carries him so far from the poem
itself that he can say that "there is no notion of revenge" in the last
six lines—an assertion demonstrably undermined by the fact that the
poem occasions it. In short, his "reading" of the poem does not arise
from the poem but from his research into its topic.
     Huttar would never have set off on his reasonable but irrelevant
and disorienting side trip if he had not assumed that, if *rebel pow'rs*
refers to the body, it cannot refer to the affections. He therefore sets
out to "prove" that it does not refer to the body. His failure to do so
and his folly in trying are demonstrated by the last phrase in his
article: "the obvious, but erroneous, assumption that 'rebbell
powres' means the 'body.'" One cannot reasonably deny that a word
or phrase has a reference that generations of careful and informed
readers have assumed it to have—unless one does so on historical
grounds, on the basis of a demonstration that in the given context
the audience for whom the work was written would not have taken
the meaning later readers take from the word or phrase in question.
One can reasonably argue that a writer's own audience would have

taken more (or more complex) meaning than we do, but to do that is not to demonstrate that a meaning obvious to us was not always obvious. Huttar introduces his quotation from Aristotle with this: "It is wrong to take 'these rebbell powres' as referring to 'the physical being' (Southam, p. 69). A contemporary reader would have seen without hesitation that this spoke of the powers of the soul." I am not at all certain about the validity of the second of those sentences; I surely do not see the probability that Shakespeare's reader would have been more aware of or more on the lookout for the Aristotelian theory of the three souls than the modern scholars who have commented on the poem; I am certain that the implied logical connection between these two sentences is illegitimate.

(The particular case of *rebel pow'rs* in Sonnet 146 both strengthens and weakens my general thesis that neither a disquisition on what a word or phrase or poem should have meant to its readers nor a demonstration that previous readings have been incomplete should be mistaken for proof that previous readings have been erroneous: *these rebel pow'rs* are said to *array* the soul, and one sense of *array* demands that the *pow'rs* be understood as the body because the body is to the soul as clothing is to the body. However, even if the reference of *pow'rs* did not demonstrably include the body, I would be loathe to assume that the scholarly consensus on *these rebel pow'rs* can be dismissed. . . .)

The kind of thinking behind Huttar's discussion of *rebel pow'rs* is not unusual in criticism, but it is surprising to find it in this critic in this article. Huttar's general assertion of poetic value is a model of sense, sensitivity, and precision: "I take it that the power to sustain a single image through a passage of several lines is of a higher order than the power to create (or borrow) a series of images, each one apt but unrelated to the others. Better yet is the poet who can sustain an image, and in the same words flash before the reader's attention the enriching association of disparate images." In the main, Huttar's practical criticism of Sonnet 146 admirably reflects those generalizations. Moreover, the stated purpose of his essay is to answer Southam's article and take him to task for making just the sort of unreasoningly reductive argument about the poem as a whole that Huttar then makes about *rebel pow'rs*.

Southam's argument progresses in the traditional manner of demonstrations that the critical history of a work is the product of an informal conspiracy to misread:

This sonnet is generally accepted as a statement of Shakespeare's sympathetic attitude towards a commonplace of Christian doctrine. The theme is understood to be a combination of "I keep under my body, and bring it into subjection" (I Cor.9.27.) and "O death, where is thy sting? O grave, where is thy victory?" (I Cor.15.55.), and the commentary and criticism on the poem reveal an impressive unanimity: Shakespeare's Christian sentiments are applauded; the clarity of expression and the absence of ambiguity are noted; and it is allowed a place among the greatest of the sequence. . . . [Southam then quotes a number of comments to demonstrate that] both scholar and ordinary reader concur. They find that Shakespeare endorses bodily subjugation as a means to spiritual health, and thereby, to a conquest of death. The sonnet is hailed as an unqualified statement of orthodox Christian belief and, as such, a unique document in the Shakespeare canon. Only once have I seen it suggested that this reading may not necessarily be definitive. In *The American Scholar*, Vol. XII, under the title "Critical Principles and a Sonnet," D. A. Stauffer records a discussion between five critics which centered upon Sonnet 146. During the course of the discussion John Crowe Ransom remarked: "I am struck by the fact that the divine terms which the soul buys are not particularly Christian: there are few words in the poem that would directly indicate conventional religious dogma. Rather, in the notion that the soul is a mere tenant of the body, a prince who has fallen to the condition of a sentinel in the world's garrison, a stranger coming from another realm, the sonnet seems in spirit to be Platonic." This comment was not amplified by Ransom, nor did his companions take it up, and although I am not able to agree with him in particulars of his criticism his overall impression that the sonnet is not merely an endorsement of Christian asceticism hints that a more penetrating reading is possible.

The crucial word in the passage is "merely" in the last sentence. Had Southam stayed with it, his essay would have had greater validity. As the comments quoted in the foregoing notes illustrate,

Southam demonstrates that quatrain 1 requires a reader to see the soul personified in several different roles and that it evokes both pity and blame for the soul. He is less detailed in describing the next two quatrains, but his focus is upon the elements in them that make a reader morally uneasy about the selfishness of the soul. In his eagerness to correct his predecessors' urgent insistence that 146 is an *uncomplicated* Christian exposition of *contemptus mundi,* he allows an argument that starts off in a demonstration that the "feeling, thought, and expression" of this poem are not in perfect harmony throughout to drift into argument that 146 is not a Christian exposition of *contemptus mundi* at all. Finally, he abandons the admirable effort at correcting an oversimplification; he replaces the oversimplification with its much less justifiable and equally reductive opposite; he finally disappears down an all-purpose critical rabbit hole by declaring an irony:

> Luce calls the sonnet "an exact epitome of the Biblical yet lofty morality of Shakespeare's time." There are, true enough, a number of Biblical echoes which superficially run the poem along a conventional course, and the values of the poem seem to be those of the prosperous Elizabethan world. But it is Shakespeare the humanist speaking, pleading for the life of the body as against the rigorous asceticism which glorifies the life of the spirit at the expense of the vitality and richness of sensuous experience. Neither spiritual nor bodily life can be fulfilled at the other's cost, for the whole man, body and spirit indivisible, will suffer thereby. We can see how very much higher is the charity which motivates this sonnet than the type of Christianity which moves on the surface of the poem, and at which the irony is directed.

One alternative to analyses that are emotionally and intellectually satisfying in their own terms but are otherwise unsatisfactory is an analysis that avoids conceding to the intellectual convenience of the critic and his readers, and therefore does not provide the satisfaction we are accustomed to getting by writing and reading criticism. Both Southam and Huttar learned from—and failed to learn the lesson of—Donald Stauffer's insufferable and invaluable memorial reconstruction of a conversation about Sonnet 146 held in the early 1940s by Reuben Brower, John Crowe Ransom, Daniel Aaron, Elizabeth Drew, and Stauffer himself. Stauffer's article admits more of the truth about Sonnet 146 than anything before or since and also comes closer than anything I know to capturing the experience of reading any great poem. It is as wholesome an example as one could set for a serious student of literature. And yet, although the distinction of the participants in the discussion should have been enough to insure a general audience for Stauffer's essay, it is omitted from most bibliographies and ignored in the anthologies of sonnet criticism by Willen and Reed and by Barbara Herrnstein—both of which contain an otherwise excellent sampling of the best criticisms available in the early 1960s and also show considerable barrel-scraping. Edward Hubler did acknowledge Stauffer's account of the conversation (*The Sense of Shakespeare's Sonnets* [N.Y., 1952]), but did so only to make fun of the participants as having ignored "Shakespeare's warning that 'they that dally nicely with words may quickly make them wanton'"; in the sanctimony of his clearheadedness Hubler forgot that, as Viola's line shows, Shakespeare was the Don Juan of verbal dalliance.

The reasons Stauffer's report has been rejected or ignored are, I think, two. The first is trivial. The essay is embarrassing to read; its style is that of a love child of James Fenimore Cooper and Geoffrey Chaucer; its format is both coyly and pedantically imitative of classical and Renaissance pastoral dialogues and also sports some trimmings from the *Symposium* of Plato. The second reason goes deeper. Reading the essay is like thinking about the sonnet, not like reading critical analyses of it. The essay tells the truth without focusing on *one* truth about the poem and subordinating the others to it.

Most critical articles leave a reader knowing more facts than he did before, but their chief achievement, function, and value is actually to allow a reader to know *less* about a work than he knew before, to excuse him from the inconvenience of admitting all of his experience of a work into his memory of it. As one reads through Stauffer's dialogue, the five critics keep questioning, modifying, negating, and dismissing each others' statements, but, except for a few rare and mentally refreshing moments of transparent nonsense, one is likely to find oneself feeling that each speaker is making, or pointing the way to, the definitive statement about the poem; each seems to be saying *the* thing one thought as one read the poem, and one forgets that one has accepted the preceding speakers' comments as equally summary. Each of the five voices tries to establish one angle of vision on the poem; each succeeds, and none can maintain its absolute truth as exclusive. The five critics keep agreeing with each other and registering surprise at the extent of their agreement; it does not seem possible to them that so many conclusive statements are not mutually exclusive. The five critics talking to each other are like a single mind at the point when it perceives the need to pick out one thread in the poem and subordinate everything else to it. Since they are five individual minds, they cannot do that. They just go home.

Stauffer packages the hodgepodge of unaccommodated truths in a narrative framework that makes the whole essay a mere literary curiosity, but had he not done so, had he not acted as an artist, packaging truth rather than trying to flatten it out and line it up on an expository grid, he would not have been able to retain all of the discussion or as much of the poem as he did. [My] notes on Sonnet 146 are a different sort of attempt to admit that all that occurs in this poem exists. The notes are not unsatisfying in the particular way that Stauffer's appear to have been, but they are surely unsatisfying. If Hubler had lived to see them, he would probably have scorned them as he scorned Stauffer's ideologically unmediated reproduction of a conversation; any critic determined to demonstrate the reasonable but mistaken assumption that a simple straightforward poem like Sonnet 146 must derive its clarity from some one expository assertion (which is embodied in it and for which the particulars of the poem are only a many-colored coat) would have to do the same. Such a critic assumes that, when someone else focuses on any incidental ideational element in a poem, he offers it as the real "point" of the poem, a substitute for the clear and clearly intended substance of the poet's sentences. As I have previously said, that is often true: critics often—critics usually—make such reductions. But that is not necessarily true, and it is particularly untrue about the five critics in Stauffer's dialogue. Whatever fears of false conclusions individual statements in that conversation may have inspired in Hubler, I suspect that his main dissatisfaction arose not from individual instances of misguided absolutism but from the inconclusiveness of the whole. The five critics never made up their minds about Sonnet 146.

The value of making up one's mind about a poem is not the same as the value of making up one's mind about real-life events that one's decision can influence. Nothing one says or thinks about a poem can change it. What one says about a poem can sometimes change the angle of a reader's perception of it, but one cannot stop the poem from doing all that it does or argue it into doing what it does not do. No interpretive description of a poem can nullify any of the actions the poem performs upon a reader's understanding. A piece of information unknown to the reader can put additional actions into the poem; so can changing its context; an historically irrelevant response (e.g., the special wit that "A True Maid" by Matthew Prior [1664–1721] can have for a reader familiar with "The Sick Rose" by William Blake [1757–1827] and the misunderstandings that flow from ignorance of the history of the word "interest" [see 74.3]) can be corrected and, perhaps, in time forgotten (although I personally find that I still must actively reject a reference to a horse when I read 127.3 and that Dickens's Mr. Guppy makes me think of an eager little fish—even though *Bleak House* was published during 1852–53, and the Reverend R. J. L. Guppy of Trinidad did not send the first recorded specimen of *lebistes reticulatus* to the British Museum until the following decade). An interpretive description can even convince a reader that some of his experience of a poem does not or should not occur, but that is not at all the same thing as actually doing away with those responses. Moreover, critics regularly admit the existence of responses they deny by the very act of arguing against them. To argue against a reading that results from an historical accident (Prior and Blake are both in our past, and we are accustomed to the idea that "to be interested in" is "to have one's attention engaged by"), or for a reading lost by a similar accident of the progress of time may not lead to perfect practical success, but such activity is surely benign in both intention and effect. Arguments against a reading that the poem evokes and that it can be legitimately argued to have evoked for its first audience are usually benign in intent (we like to know exactly what something is and what it is not), but they are not benign in effect: such criticisms leave a reader with a clearer sense of what the poem means than the poem itself ever gave; such criticisms are intellectually comforting—but only so long as the reader does not go back and reread the poem on which he now has so firm a grasp.

It is as unreasonable and unprofitable to argue that Sonnet 146 does not espouse an orthodox Christian position on the relative value of mortal and immortal considerations as it is to deny that the poem generates the ideational static Ransom and Southam point out.

That brings us to another familiar and inviting way of packaging disparate truths: I would not want to recommend any account of this poem that called it a Christian exhortation tempered by, or modified by, other considerations; to do so would be to recommend homogenizing the experience of the poem. It would be intellectually convenient to say that the standard descriptions of this poem as a straightforward exercise in Christian resolve are products of wishful thinking, but the fact that such critical descriptions protest too much attests not only to the presence of other and complicating elements in the poem but *also* to the fact that the poem itself evokes those descriptions; that is to say that Sonnet 146 *is* the simple unalloyed exhortation it is said to be and that those of its details which make such descriptions difficult (make it necessary to sprinkle one's descriptions with words like "surely," "obviously," "unqualified," and "unambiguous," and to insist on the poem's undeniable likeness to Sidney's "Leave me o Love"), coexist with the obvious statement of religious resolve but do not diminish its force, simplicity, or single-mindedness. It does not seem reasonable that such a coexistence should be possible, that the elements would not immediately resolve themselves in a mixture comparable to the one that results from mixing black paint and white paint, or that the critic's job would be other than determining the proportions of black to white and thus the particular shade of gray. However, the incompatible elements, points of view, and responses do retain their independence, do not undergo synthesis. Such improbable coexistence occurs regularly in human experience: take, for example, the idea of "love-hate" relationships so popular with amateur psychologists. The sonnets regularly take such paradoxical situations for topics and reproduce them in the reader rather than resolving them. If the 1609 sequence has a common denominator it is the unity of divisible things and the divisibility of units; the speaker repeatedly presents his reader with things that at once have an absolute identity and just as absolutely do not.

I have attached this editorial plea to my annotation of Sonnet 146 because its topic—the total unification of separable spiritual elements (reason, passions) as one element in a unified pair of separable elements (soul, body), which are distinguishable as immortal and mortal and are each also both immortal and mortal—is one of the few topics where the human mind has traditionally been most urgently unsuccessful in pacifying itself by the rational exercise of categories and subordination. One of my purposes in annotating the sonnets is to recommend an unmediated analysis of works of art (or an analysis that at least tries to resist mediation), an analysis that is not satisfying in anything like the way its subject is satisfying, an analysis that does not try to decide which of a poem's actions should be acknowledged but instead tries to explain the means by which all a poem's improbably sorted actions coexist and cohere within the poem and, for the duration of the poem, within the mind of its reader. If I am to have any success, Sonnet 146 is the proper place to make my plea. The idea of the soul as a politic, parasitic exploiter of the body should seem ridiculous; all the traditions of Western culture make us reject the implications that the metaphors of master and servant, landlord and tenant bring with them. As presented in Sonnet 146, the relationships of master and servant, and of landlord and tenant are simply not analogous to the relationship of soul to body. Yet we are used to these metaphors as vehicles for discussing the relationship of the mortal and immortal parts of human beings; these metaphors are the Bible's own, and they do not ordinarily give us trouble. Moreover, the speaker gives us no hint that we are to view the argument here as any less noble than we are used to finding it. The last line, in fact, is moving in its serenity. Sonnet 146 is, as readers have traditionally thought, a Christian exhortation to reject transient pleasures and gain eternal life. As we read the poem we know we are reading a traditional statement of *contemptus mundi*. As we read the poem we see the relation of body and soul as our impressions of Christian doctrine (rather than a course of study in St. Paul) make us expect to see it. The speaker uses the traditional metaphors for vivifying the relationship and enabling us to see things in a single frame of reference; he achieves *exactly* the effect we would expect such a poem to have; *and* (not *but*) he lets the metaphors of servant and master, tenant and landlord run free to evoke the responses that those relationships evoke when they are not limited by an illustrative purpose but are real business relationships between human beings who try to exploit and avoid being exploited. That is to say that 146 enables us single-mindedly to espouse spiritual values and to do so in a genuinely narrow vision that genuinely includes pertinent reminders of the considerations and attitudes it successfully excludes; 146 achieves a genuinely restricted frame of reference that *feels* as all-inclusive as the logic of Christianity asks us to believe it is.

The great virtue of poetic embodiments of human experiences is that they house undeniable contrarieties of response instead of translating experience into thesis, antithesis, and synthesis. There should therefore be reason to value a criticism that offers complex descriptions of complex objects. Why should we take it as the critic's job to deny the poem's achievement? Why should we argue that the elements that cohere in a poem are by nature any more or less compatible with one another than they ordinarily are when the poem is read by an informed reader (i.e., a reader in command of as much of the mental furniture of the poet's contemporaries as we can discover and recondition)? A criticism that denies its audience the comfort Joseph offered Pharoah and his servants when he interpreted their dreams as coded messages offers the comfort of admitting that great poems, not being god-made, do not dissolve under the ministrations of prophets. A criticism that can admit the justice of John Benson's confidence that readers of Shakespeare's poems will "finde them, seren, cleere and eligantly plaine, such gentle straines as shall recreate and not perplexe your braine, no intricate or cloudy stuffe to puzzell intellect, but perfect eloquence" (from the preface to *Poems: Written by Wil. Shakespeare,* 1640), and can *also* admit that the complexities modern critics see in the Sonnets are there and that their discoverers cannot justly be dismissed as ingenious unless they try to convert the Sonnets into mere vehicles for elements they are themselves surprised to discover—a criticism that admits that arguments for dating the Sonnets by reference to English history or to the themes and styles of the various plays, the belief in a lost original order of the Sonnets, the quasi-alchemical efforts to restore it, the expeditions to find "Mr. W. H." and "The Rival Poet," and the games of pin the tail on "The Dark Lady" have all been failures, and that admits that the Sonnets and their interrelations in the 1609 sequence constantly tempt the mind toward similar follies—such a criticism may ask more tolerance and greater patience than is convenient, but, since the usual alternatives offer their comforting illumination by temporarily darkening all but a selected few of the lights in a sonnet or in the sequence, the unsatisfying criticism I propose may be worth trying. We have tried to come to terms with the Sonnets by seeing them in light of this or in light of that. I suggest that we try coming to terms with them in all the terms they bring with them, that we attempt and attempt to tolerate a criticism that is genuinely, literally, conservative.

Pitiful Thrivers: Failed Husbandry in the Sonnets

Thomas M. Greene

Sonnet 125 of Shakespeare's collection ("Wer't ought to me I bore the canopy") is the penultimate poem in the series addressed to the male friend. It is the last complete sonnet in this series, and in comparison with its somewhat slighter successor, 126, it appears to offer a more substantial, dense, and conclusive instrument of retrospection. It opens by distinguishing the poet from those who court his friend's love by means of external gestures, "dwellers on forme and favor," but who see their calculations fail and are condemned to admire the young man from a distance: "Pittifull thrivors in their gazing spent." The poet's own devotion, he claims, consists purely of uncalculated internal gestures and it leads to a genuine, unmediated exchange.

> Noe, let me be obsequious in thy heart,
> And take thou my oblacion, poore but free,
> Which is not mixt with seconds, knows no art,
> But mutuall render onely me for thee.

The couplet dismisses a "subbornd *Informer*," a slanderer who might accuse the poet himself of dwelling on form. But despite this calumny, the affirmation of the "mutuall render" between the two men acquires in the context of the whole collection a peculiar resonance. It can be regarded as a culminating moment in the twisting history

From *Shakespeare and the Question of Theory*, edited by Patricia Parker and Geoffrey H. Hartman. © 1985 by Thomas M. Greene. Methuen, 1985.

of their relationship, and our understanding of the outcome of the "plot" in Sonnets 1–126 depends in part on our interpretation of this phrase. Contrariwise, fully to grasp the implications of the phrase and the sonnet requires consideration of all that precedes, and even to some degree what follows. An informed reading will necessitate a long swing backward before returning to 125.

Within its immediate context, this is the third of three successive sonnets affirming that the poet's love for his friend is untouched by external accidents. This succession (Sonnets 123–25) needs to be read in the light of an earlier group (109–12) alluding to the poet's shameful and scandalous conduct and another group (117–21) alluding to the poet's apparent neglect and betrayal of the friend. Thus, if one attributes validity to the Quarto sequence, the three protests of uncalculating devotion follow almost directly an experience of partial rupture, and they attempt to cement a reconciliation which has been to some degree in doubt.

But from a wider perspective, Sonnet 125 is responding to problems raised from the very opening of the collection. Its resolution of pure exchange could be said to respond to the anxiety of cosmic and existential economics which haunts the Sonnets and which marks their opening line: "From fairest creatures we desire increase." The paronomasia which links the two nouns translates phonetically the poet's obsessive concern with metaphorical wealth, profit, worth, value, expense, "store," "content." The "pittifull thrivors" of 125 take their place in a line of disappointed or misguided would-be thrivers distributed throughout the work. The "mutuall render," if in fact it is successful, would thus bring to a happy conclusion a quest for an adequate economic system which would avoid the "wast or ruining" and the excessive "rent" which burden those in 125 who vainly spend themselves. Up to the climactic reciprocity at the close of that sonnet, the sequence to the young man has provided very little by way of stable exchange systems.

The first of the pitiful thrivers is the onanistic friend as he appears in the opening seventeen "procreation" sonnets. By refusing to marry and to beget children, he "makst wast in niggarding" (Sonnet 1); he becomes a "profitles userer" "having traffike with [him] selfe alone" (Sonnet 4). The procreation sonnets display with particular brilliance Shakespeare's ability to manipulate words which in his language belonged both to the economic and the sexual/biological semantic fields: among others, "increase," "use," "spend," "free," "live," "dear," "house," "usury," "endowed," along with their cognates. The umbrella-pun which covers them all, and which establishes a semantic node for the whole collection, lies in still another word: "husbandry":

> For where is she so faire whose un-eard wombe
> Disdaines the tillage of thy husbandry?
>
> (Sonnet 3)

The ad hoc meaning "marriage" joins the traditional meanings of "thrift," "estate management," "agriculture," and, by means of a conventional metaphor, coition as ploughing. When the pun returns ten sonnets later, the dominant meaning will emerge as management:

> Who lets so faire a house fall to decay,
> Which husbandry in honour might uphold,
> Against the stormy gusts of winters day
> And barren rage of deaths eternall cold?
>
> (Sonnet 13)

"House" means both the friend's body (the *banhus,* "bonehouse," of the Anglo-Saxon kenning) and the family line. The bourgeois poet accuses the aristocratic friend of a dereliction of those responsibilities incumbent on the land-owning class. The apparent implication is that through marriage the friend could "live" (Sonnet 4), could make a profit by perpetuating his family.

But if, in the procreation sonnets, thriving seems ostensibly within the young man's grasp, one must recognize nonetheless the disproportionate force of the thwarting power, the "barren rage of deaths eternall cold." Procreation progressively comes to appear as a desperate defense, a final maneuver against a principle which is ultimately irresistible.

> And nothing gainst Times sieth [scythe] can make defence
> Save breed to brave him, when he takes thee hence.
>
> (Sonnet 12)

The recurrent terror of "winters wragged hand" (Sonnet 6), particularly notable in this opening group, comes to cast doubt on the viability of marriage. Or rather, in view of the threatening "barenes everywhere" (Sonnet 5), husbandry emerges as a universal, existential concern that transcends the addressee's marital status. It even becomes a concern of the poetry we are reading, which alternately promises to "ingraft" the friend anew in the war with Time (Sonnet 15) only to describe itself as "barren" in the sequel (Sonnet 16). The friend, "making a famine where aboundance lies" (Sonnet 1), may after all be closer to the governing principle of the world, in which case the poet and his poetry are left in a confusing limbo.

Thus a terrible fear of cosmic destitution overshadows the husbandry of the procreation sonnets, a fear in excess of the announced argument, not easily circumscribed, rendering the bourgeois desire for "store" more urgent, eccentric, and obsessive. In the main body of the sonnets to the young man (Sonnets 18–126), this fear continues to find frequent expression but it is also localized much more explicitly in the poet's feelings about himself. The poetry reflects a sense of inner depletion, emptiness, poverty, which the friend is asked or stated to fill up; elsewhere it reflects a nakedness which the friend is asked to clothe. Sometimes the language evoking the friend's role might suggest literal patronage; elsewhere it might suggest a literal filling up through sex; but each of these literalizations taken alone would reduce the quality of the expressed need. The sense of depletion is more radical and more diffuse, and it is inseparable from feelings of worthlessness and deprivation. Sonnet 29 ("When in disgrace with Fortune") represents the speaker

> Wishing me like to one more rich in hope,
> Featur'd like him, like him with friends possest,
> Desiring this mans art, and that mans skope,
> With what I most inioy contented least.

The language faintly underscores the economic character of this despondency. Friends, if they existed, would be possessed. "Rich in hope" means both "endowed with hope" and "rich in prospect." "Inioy" here means "possess" as well as "take pleasure in" ([Stephen] Booth), thus justifying a secondary reading of "contented least": "poorest in whatever I own of worth." This privation is only relieved by thoughts of the friend: "thy sweet love remembred . . . welth brings," and this transfer is dramatized by the imagistic wealth of the lark simile interrupting the rhetorical bareness of the octave. In the following sonnet, 30 ("When to the Sessions"), the poet laments the deaths of precious friends, moans the expense of many a vanished sight, pays anew "the sad account of fore-bemoned mone," until with remembrance of his friend "all losses are restord, and sorrowes end." In Sonnet 26 ("Lord of my love"), the poet sends his naked poetry as an offering to his liege lord, hoping that the friend will dress the drab language in "some good conceit of thine," will "[put] apparell on my tottered loving." Dressing the tottered (tattered) loving might mean making the poet more eloquent or more rich or more accomplished as a lover, but the nakedness seems finally to transcend rhetoric or money or seductiveness. In Sonnet 38 ("How can my Muse"), the friend is once again filling a void:

> How can my Muse want subiect to invent
> While thou dost breath that poor'st into my verse
> Thine own sweet argument?

The friend plays the masculine role, pouring his worth into the otherwise barren verse, leaving the poet with the travail of giving birth but rightly taking credit for any success: "The paine be mine, but thine shal be the praise." In this economic system, all value seems to reside in the friend, or in *thoughts* of the friend, and the poet seems to be a leaky vessel constantly in need of replenishing, his personal and linguistic poverty never definitively abolished.

This system, however, rests on a shaky basis. The worth of the friend may reside after all in the poet's own fancy, as at least one passage may be understood to suggest:

> So then I am not lame, poore, nor dispis'd,
> Whilst that this shadow doth such substance give,
> That I in thy abundance am suffic'd.
>
> (Sonnet 37)

The substance of abundance may actually derive from the shadow of projection. This doubt becomes more plausible as fears of betrayal mount

> Thou best of deerest, and mine onely care,
> Art left the prey of every vulgar theefe
>
> (Sonnet 48)

and as the fears are realized in the young man's affair with the poet's mistress (Sonnets 40–42): "Both finde each other, and I loose both twaine" (Sonnet 42). In other sonnets apparently free of jealousy, a threat to the friend's worth looms from the cosmic mutability already evoked in the procreation sonnets, and now an alternative economic system situates the source of value in the poetry of the Sonnets. The poetry, elsewhere naked, becomes in these poems an artifact that successfully resists time and death, assures eternal life to the one it celebrates, distills his truth for the ages, acts as a perpetuating force against "mortall rage" (Sonnet 64). In the sonnets which affirm this source of value, the young man is represented as a potential victim, helpless against the cosmic principle of destruction, passive, disarmed, doomed without the saving power of "my verse." Verse preserves, engrafts, refurbishes; it seems informed with a masculine force the friend lacks. He remains in this system the beneficiary of a gift his worth draws to itself, but this worth is not otherwise active. "Where alack, shall times best Iewell from times chest lie hid?" (Sonnet 65). The young man's excellence is a plunderable commodity, as it is elsewhere perishable; inert as a precious stone, it belongs to the world of basic elements in flux, "increasing store with losse, and losse with store" (Sonnet 64). The alleged source of genuine "store" in this class of sonnets is the poetry.

Yet it is noteworthy that the affirmations of this linguistic power tend to appear in the couplets of these sonnets (15, 18, 19, 54, 60, 63, 65; exceptions are 55 and 81). The couplets, moreover, tend to lack the energy of the negative vision in the twelve lines that precede them. The final affirmation in its flaccidity tends to refute itself; the *turn* fails to reverse the rhetorical momentum adequately, as the language loses its wealth and its potency while asserting them.

> His beautie shall in these blacke lines be seene,
> And they shall live, and he in them still greene.
>
> (Sonnet 63)

> O none, unlesse this miracle have might,
> That in black inck my love may still shine bright.
>
> (Sonnet 65)

The turn toward restoration can be read as a desperate bourgeois maneuver, struggling to shore up the cosmic economy against the mutability which instigates true verbal power. The poetry arguably fails to celebrate, refurbish the worth of the young man. The worth remains abstract, faceless, blurred, even when it is not tainted.

Thus we are left with two distinct sources of alleged value, the friend and the poetry, each the basis for a rudimentary economic system, each vulnerable to skepticism. The presence of each system tends to destabilize the other by casting doubt on the kind of value it attempts to establish. To cite the poetic convention behind each system does not adequately deal with its constituent presence in this work. At stake in this conflict of systems is the status and force of the poetic word, which alternately shares its maker's hollowness and serves his (narcissistic?) fantasies of power. The one system, the one relationship which is *not* to be found before the last sonnets to the friend is equal, direct, unmediated reciprocity. Reciprocity is unattainable partly because of the poet's social inferiority and, so to speak, his felt "human" inferiority, because the friend frequently appears in thought, fantasy, or memory rather than in the flesh, because the adulatory style intermittently gives way to suspicion, resentment, fear, anger (Sonnets 33–35, 40–42, 57–58, 67, 69, etc.) which militate negatively against equality, because the friend as an individual remains a "shadow," undescribed, voiceless, hazy, dehumanized by the very superlatives he attracts, and because the poetry, however unclear its status, is repeatedly presented as the binding agent of mediation, an essential go-between. It is not clear whether *any* of the Sonnets is to be read as a spoken address, a dramatic monologue, rather than as a written communication. Many of them refer to themselves as written, refer to paper, ink, pens, and to poetic style. They may occasionally affirm a closeness between poet and friend, but their very existence suggests a distance which has to be crossed. We are never allowed to envision unambiguously the poet in the presence of his friend, as we are in love poems by Wyatt, Sidney, Spenser, and Donne.

The conflicting representations of the poetry's power (potent or weak?), its gender (male or female?), its durability (perennial or transient?) together with its mediating function between the two men raise questions about what might be called its rhetorical economics. The poetry is distinguished by its supercharged figurative density, its inexhaustible ramifications of suggestion, its insidious metaphoric multiplications, a superfetation which might have been accumulated to avoid at all cost the alleged danger of nakedness. The poetry could be working to refute its own self-accusations of dearth and repetition.

> Why is my verse so barren of new pride?
> So far from variation or quicke change?
>
> . . . .
> So all my best is dressing old words new,
> Spending againe what is already spent.
>
> (Sonnet 76)

As though to adorn the monotony, every rift is loaded with ore, to the degree that the rhetorical density can be read as an extraordinary effort to exorcize that stylistic poverty the poetry imputes to itself. The poet may feel himself to be depleted, but he evidently owns enough wit to spend it extravagantly. Yet this very supercharging of language tends to heighten a certain impression of linguistic slippage. Metaphors are mixed, replaced by others, recalled, jostled, interfused, inverted, disguised, dangled, eroded, in ways which blur meanings as they are enriched.

> Nativity once in the maine of light,
> Crawles to maturity, wherewith being crown'd,
> Crooked eclipses gainst his glory fight,
> And time that gave, doth now his gift confound.
>
> (Sonnet 60)

The enriching of metaphor, a putative demonstration of the poet's real potency, is indistinguishable from a mutability of metaphor, a fragmentation which might be said to demonstrate instability. By this reading the process of verbal enrichment would coincide with a process of deterioration; indeed the enrichment might be perceived as leading to the slippage, "increasing store with losse, and losse with store." The poetry would then come to resemble a pail of the Danaids, and the questions regarding the poet's potency would remain open.

That poetic potency is related here to sexual potency is made clear beyond cavil by the rival poet group (Sonnets 78–80, 82–86). The other poet is a rival both for patronage and for sexual favors, and his rhetorical brilliance (or bombast) is associated with his glittering seductiveness. Thus the poetic speaker is doubly threatened by "the proud full saile of his great verse, bound for the prize of (al to precious) you" (Sonnet 86). The revealing word here is *proud,* which meant "lecherous" as well as "stately" and "ostentatious." Cognate forms have already appeared in Sonnet 80, which constitutes a tissue of sexual double meanings and interweaves poetic competition inextricably with erotic:

> O how I faint when I of you do write,
> Knowing a better spirit doth use your name,
> And in the praise thereof spends all his might,
> To make me toung-tide speaking of your fame.
> But since your worth (wide as the Ocean is)

> The humble as the proudest saile doth beare,
> My sawsie barke (inferior farre to his)
> On your broad maine doth wilfully appeare.
> Your shallowest helpe will hold me up a floate,
> Whilst he upon your soundlesse deepe doth ride,
> Or (being wrackt) I am a worthlesse bote,
> He of tall building, and of goodly pride.
> > Then if he thrive and I be cast away,
> > The worst was this, my love was my decay.

So many words have sexual meanings ("use," "spends," "proudest," "saucy," "wilfully," "ride," "pride"—by attraction, "tall building") that the reader is tempted to interpret the sonnet primarily in erotic terms. But it opens with a contrast of the rivals as writers before shifting in lines 11–12 to a presumptive contrast of physical endowments. It is true that the analogy of the possibly promiscuous love object with the ocean will return more crudely and unambiguously in the dark lady group (Sonnet 134). But if language is presented in Sonnet 80 as a means to seduction, seduction on the other hand may consist simply of verbal overpowering. "Love" and poetic language are linked so closely that the primary meaning of the final clause would seem to be "my inadequate verse has led to my rejection." The contrast of the rivals underscores what the speaker will shortly call his *penury,* a word which brings together his financial, poetic, and sexual shortcomings but which leaves uncertain what is figure and what ground. At any rate the rival, however we regard his challenge, introduces a complicating factor in the economics of the Sonnets, by appearing to "thrive" (Sonnet 80, l. 13) while the speaker is ruined. In spending more, verbally, sartorially, and sexually, he may get more. Yet in the end he and his new patron will be revealed as devalued, the one by the vulgarity of his praise and the other by the vulgarity of the pleasure he takes in it. They are pitiful thrivers both. So at least the poet suggests, and he follows the rival poet group with a temporary kiss-off, not without sarcasm:

> Farewell thou art too deare for my possessing,
> And like enough thou knowst thy estimate.
>
> (Sonnet 87)

Farewell also to the theme of poetry's immortalizing power: with two brief exceptions (Sonnets 100, 107), it will disappear from the collection.

The rival poet group is of interest because it confirms the implicit linkage between monetary, verbal, and sexual "pride," and because it complicates the linkage between these forms of power and deeper, vaguer intrinsic "worth." The group is equally of interest because it throws up, almost incidentally, a revealing formulation of the Sonnets' essential vulnerability, a formulation which will prove useful when we return to our starting point in Sonnet 125:

> Who is it that sayes most, which can say more,
> Then this rich praise, that you alone, are you,
> In whose confine immured is the store,
> Which should example where your equall grew,
> Leane penurie within that Pen doth dwell,
> That to his subiect lends not some small glory,
> But he that writes of you, if he can tell,
> That you are you, so dignifies his story.
> Let him but coppy what in you is writ.
>
> (Sonnet 84)

The pen is penurious which cannot add to its subject, but a praiser of the friend is subject to this penury, since in him "are locked up all the qualities needed to provide an equal example." The friend's alleged excellence is such that no metaphors are available, no imagistic equivalent is possible, and the authentic praiser will limit himself to pure representation ("Let him but coppy"). Only by representing accurately, achieving a perfect counterpart of the young man, will the poet overcome penury, "making his stile admired every where." But this last solution, in its context, proves to be unsatisfactory on several grounds. First it fails to escape epideictic drabness, by the poet's own showing. It leaves the poetry "barren of new pride," spending again the respent, "keep[ing] invention in a noted weed" (Sonnet 76). Second, he who is to be copied proves to be less of a Platonic idea than a changeable and fallible human; for that revelation we need go no further than the couplet of this sonnet (84), with its malicious glance at the rival's demeaning flattery.

> You to your beautious blessings adde a curse,
> Being fond on praise, which makes your praises worse.

A certain pathology of praise can infect both parties. But the third and most momentous reason why the copy solution fails is that pure representation in language is not of this world. Poetry depends on figuration, but precise figural adequation is unattainable. What is said with ostensible hyperbole in the opening quatrain—that no "example" can serve as "equall" to the young man—is universally true. To attempt not to add to one's subject may court penury, as Sonnet 84 argues, but the real failure lies in the necessity of accepting addition, of employing "compounds strange" (Sonnet 76), as the Sonnets most decidedly do and as all poetry does. Poetry as representation will always be vulnerable, because in its shifting mass of meanings it can never copy with absolute precision and because that which is copied changes, gains, and loses value. The economics of copying reserves its own pitfalls for aspirant thrivers; the pen is bound to be penurious.

Sonnet 105 betrays a similar vulnerability:

> Let not my love be cal'd Idolatrie,
> Nor my beloved as an Idoll show,
> Since all alike my songs and praises be
> To one, of one, still such, and ever so.
> Kinde is my love to day, to morrow kinde,
> Still constant in a wondrous excellence,
> Therefore my verse to constancie confin'de,
> One thing expressing, leaves out difference.
> Faire, kinde, and true, is all my argument,
> Faire, kinde and true, varrying to other words,
> And in this change is my invention spent,
> Three theams in one, which wondrous scope affords.
>> Faire, kinde, and true, have often liv'd alone.
>> Which three till now, never kept seate in one.

This appears to be another apology for an allegedly plain style. (I follow [W. G.] Ingram and [Theodore] Redpath in interpreting "since" in line 3 as introducing the reason for the accusation, not its defense; the latter begins in line 5.) Although the poet claims to hew single-mindedly to a unique theme with the same constant language, he cannot, he says, be accused of idolatry because the friend, in his inalterable generosity, deserves no less. The poetry "leaves out difference," spending its invention by varying three words in others. One might argue that *some* difference is already present in this variation. But there are differences in the word "difference" itself, as one learns from a glance at Booth's paragraph on the word; among its relevant meanings are "variety," "anything else," "disagreement," "hostility." *Constant* means both "invariable" and "faithful"; *kinde* means both "generous" and "true to his own nature"; *spent,* that ubiquitous word, means both "used" and "exhausted." The Sonnets escape the charge of idolatry, not because the man they celebrate remains correspondingly unchanging (he is nothing if not inconstant, in both senses), but because they fail to express one thing and systematically admit difference. They alternately valorize and deplore a plain stylistic constancy which they cannot achieve.

The problem of "difference," like the related problem of accurate representation, is pertinent to the affirmation of mutuality which concludes the long section of sonnets to the young man. Before we reach that affirmation, we hear of derelictions on both sides, derelictions grave enough to undermine the fragile economic systems in force earlier. The falsity of the friend, a mansion of vices (Sonnet 95), produces a policy of husbandry the precise reverse of that recommended in the procreation sonnets; now it is those who remain aloof from others like a stone who "husband natures ritches from expence" (Sonnet 94). The poet for his part has made himself a motley to the view, "sold cheap what is most deare" (Sonnet 110), blemished himself and his love. We have already noted the waning of poetry's asserted power as an immortalizing agent. As the Sonnets spiral downward in a vortex of betrayal, counter-betrayal, and justifications not untouched with sophistry, we look for an economic alternative to mere self-deception, that "alcumie . . . creating every bad a perfect best" (Sonnet 114). Something like this alternative can be glimpsed briefly in Sonnet 120, where the mutuality of suffering and dishonor might produce mutual guilt in compassion and lead to an exchange of quasi-Christian redemption:

> But that your trespasse now becomes a fee,
> Mine ransoms yours, and yours must ransome mee.

This glimpse of reciprocity in shared weakness fades, however, and leads to the group of three (Sonnets 123–25) with which we began, a group essentially protesting the poet's freedom from self-interest and the enduring purity of his feelings, which will never flag and can dispense with ostentatious demonstrations. The last of this group culminates in the proffered "mutuall render" between poet and friend, before the very last poem to the friend, 126, returns to the theme of time and anticipates nature's final, mortal settling of accounts: "her *Quietus* is to render thee."

A skeptical reading of these concluding gambits would represent them as repressing artificially the pain and guilt which have already surfaced, and which will surface even more harshly in the dark lady group to follow. In their context these protests of fidelity, which "nor growes with heat, nor drownes with showres" (Sonnet 124), could be regarded as attempts to mask the real bankruptcy of the relationship. The negative stress of Sonnets 123–25, lingering over that change (123), "policy" (124), form (125) the poet abjures, might well be read as symptomatic of a bad conscience whose spokesman would be the (internal) accusatory informer of 125. This repressive character of the final sonnets could plausibly be linked to their return to a relatively aureate style after the burst of directness earlier (as in Sonnet 120—"y'have past a hell of Time"). This *suspicion* of the excessive protest does hang over the concluding group, deepened by their conspicuous discontinuity with their context. Yet a purely cynical reading would strain out that element of real wishing which is also present. The reader can recognize the implausibility of the asserted constancy while regarding the struggle to hope, the conative pathos, with respect.

The crucial sonnet in this group is 125, since it seems to offer at last the possibility of a stable existential economics, a definitive end to penury, a compensation for the expense of living and feeling, even though it does this like its predecessors in large part by exclusion:

> Wer't ought to me I bore the canopy,
> With my extern the outward honoring,
> Or layd great bases for eternity,
> Which proves more short then wast or ruining?
> Have I not seene dwellers on forme and favor
> Lose all, and more by paying too much rent
> For compound sweet; Forgoing simple savor,
> Pittifull thrivors in their gazing spent.
> Noe, let me be obsequious in thy heart,
> And take thou my oblacion, poore but free,
> Which is not mixt with seconds, knows no art,
> But mutuall render onely me for thee.
>> Hence, thou subbornd *Informer,* a trew soule
>> When most impeacht, stands least in thy controule.

Lines 1–12 are ostensibly responding to the calumny of the unidentified informer of line 13, a calumny whose content we can determine only through its refutation. This consists in a repudiation of what might be called affective formalism, external gestures of dutifulness like the carrying of a canopy of state over a monarch's head. Suitors who employ such external gestures may believe that they prepare in this way for an everlasting intimacy with him whose favor they court, but the intimacy "paradoxically turns out to be briefer than the time required to run through an estate by extravagance" (Ingram and Redpath, [*Shakespeare's Sonnets*]). We have still another example of failed husbandry, combining formalism with the kind of decadent sophistication which would prefer cloying elaborate sauces ("compound sweet") to the familiar taste of homely fare. *Forme* (l. 5) brings together the young man's physical figure, the ceremonial of line 1, exaggerated courtesy, hollow gestures of servility, and the craft which produces "compound sweet," artificial confections of any sort, but which is allegedly absent from the poet's oblation. "Compound sweet" recalls the poetic "compounds strange" of Sonnet 76, which the poet there reproached himself for omitting from his own verse. This suggests that dwellers on form are also ambitious poets whose style is overwrought. The image of the projected manor house (l. 3) is faintly sustained by "ruining" (l. 4), "dwellers" (l. 5), "rent" (l. 6), and the possible allusion to compound and simple interest (l. 7). This version of negative formalism ends with the loaded word "spent" (l. 8), in which so much meaning has sedimented throughout the work; here it means "bankrupted," "exhausted," "failed," ironically "summed up" in reliance on visual externals, and doubtless also "drained of semen," as the suitors' sexual designs are reduced to voyeurism. Unsuccessful entrepreneurs, with only the groundworks built of their mansion of love, the failure of their misguided, formalist generosity is symbolized by the suitors' symbolic distance from their prize, observable but not touchable.

Lines 9–12 supply the poet's redemptive version of erotic ceremonial, which substitutes the eucharistic oblation for the canopied court procession. In this secularized sacrament, the dutiful ("obsequious") poet freely makes an offering intended to manifest the inwardness and simplicity of his own devotion, knowing, or thinking that he knows, that his oblation will win him the unmediated, inner reciprocity which is his goal. The oblation which "knows no art," free from the charge of formalism, is that poetry which, as in Sonnet 105, is confined to constancy, "to one, of one, still such, and ever so." Just as in 105 it "leaves out difference," in 125 it "is not mixt with seconds." Yet ironically and pathetically, the word "oblacion" is mixed with a transcendent "second," the deity of the communion service, so that the metaphor can only be regarded as a very strange, and somewhat ambiguous, compound. The use of the sacramental term leaves the reader uncertain just how much weight to accord it, and, by introducing the unbridgeable hierarchy of human and divine, would seem to annul in advance the pure reciprocity of the "mutuall render." To deny the operation of art requires art, and this art will prohibit the reciprocal affective mutuality toward which the whole work has seemed to want to move. To compose poetry is expensive, just as loving is expensive, and the unformulated implication of the work as a whole seems to be that expense is never truly recuperated. The increase we desire from fairest creatures never materializes. Spending leaves one spent, and it fails to buy immediacy; it places a residue of compound feeling and compound language between lover and beloved. Here in Sonnet 125 the very word "seconds" is a compound. It means primarily "merchandise of inferior quality," but it associates itself with the "compound sweet" and thus with that formalist craft from which the oblation is supposedly pure. But banning "seconds" from his poetry, the poet introduces a "second," which is to say a metaphor, and one which is complicated with still more implications. Language is condemned to be compound; poetry *is* art; it shapes and forms and distorts; it introduces inequalities, like the inequality between an offering and an exchange, or the inequality between a secular offering and the sacramental body of Christ.

Thus neither a "pure" offering (Booth discerns this "second" meaning in the word "poore") nor a pure mutuality is possible in a relationship which depends on the word; still less is it possible when the word, as here, is always presented as written. In a curious sonnet which immediately precedes the group 123–25, the poet reports that he has given away a gift he had received from the friend. This gift had been a notebook, "tables." It is unclear whether the notebook contained writing by the friend or memorials of the relationship by the poet, or had been so intended by the giver but been allowed to remain blank. The stress in any case falls on the superior retentiveness of the poet's mind and heart, in contrast to the limits of the "tables":

That poore retention could not so much hold,
Nor need I tallies thy deare love to skore.

(Sonnet 122)

To dispose of the notebook which contained or might have contained a written record suggests a deep dissatisfaction with language as a mediating instrument. The verb "to skore," to keep a tally, is used contemptuously, as though to insinuate that writing involves a petty arithmetic of feeling. What is striking is that the writing before us has done precisely that, has supplied us with the tallies of an intimate cost accounting. The phrase in Sonnet 122 may be scornful, and yet both inside and outside the poetic fiction the language of the poetry is all we have, keeping the score and keeping an ambiguous distance open between the tarnished lovers. As that space widens, the poet begins to look like the dwellers on form and favor, spent in his gazing across a distance. He and perhaps the friend as well become pitiful thrivers, barred from the absolute immediacy at least one of them yearns for, because poetry can never be idolatrously one and can never find the metaphor, the "example," which knows no difference. The poet's real enemy is not the "informer" as slanderer, but the voice within himself through whose forming action feeling comes into being.

In the sonnets to the dark lady that follow, poetic language is thematized less prominently; the poet's sense of inner poverty modulates to self-contempt; the physiological meanings of such words as "expense" and "will" are foregrounded. The mistress, who has "robd others beds revenues of their rents" (Sonnet 142), is perhaps the one thriver in the work who is not pitiful. Her role is antithetical to the young man's of the procreation sonnets; she is a "usurer that put'st forth all to use" (Sonnet 134) and her wealth is like the ocean's:

> The sea all water, yet receives raine still,
> And in aboundance addeth to his store,
> So thou beeing rich in *Will* adde to thy *Will*,
> One will of mine to make thy large *Will* more.
>
> (Sonnet 135)

But this inflationary economy leads to a depreciation of all values, and the only feasible policy apparently lies in a Christian husbandry:

> Why so large cost having so short a lease,
> Dost thou upon thy fading mansion spend?
>
> . . . .
>
> Buy tearmes divine in selling houres of drosse:
> Within be fed, without be rich no more.
>
> (Sonnet 146)

By the close of the sequence, however, the poet does not seem to have adopted this policy. In his disgust with sexuality and his own revolting entrapment in it, the poet tries systematically to subvert his own authority as poet and his perception of metaphoric congruence:

> O Me! what eyes hath love put in my head,
> Which have no correspondence with true sight.
>
> (Sonnet 148)

Language is systematically vulgarized, "abhored," and in the last regular sonnet to the mistress (152) the coherence of the poetic consciousness and the integrity of the poetic statement are simultaneously denied, as though the poetry had no legitimate source:

> For I have sworne thee faire; more periurde eye,
> To swere against the truth so foule a lie.

The "eye" is perjured, but also the "I" and the "aye," the capacity to affirm. "Loves eye is not so true as all mens: no" (Sonnet 148). It is as though the pitiless obscenity, love-denying and love-blaspheming, had to expose the *pudenda* of language to register the meanness of the seamy loyalties and tawdry bargains.

The Sonnets can be read to the end as attempts to cope with progressively powerful and painful forms of cost and expense. The bourgeois desire to balance cosmic and human budgets seems to be thwarted by a radical flaw in the universe, in emotion, in value, and in language. This flaw is already acted out at the beginning by the onanistic friend who "feed'st thy lights flame with selfe substantiall fewell" (Sonnet 1). In Sonnet 73, the metaphoric fire lies in its ashes as on a deathbed, "consum'd with that which it was nurrisht by." This becomes, in the terrible Sonnet 129, "a blisse in proofe and proud and very wo," a line always, unnecessarily, emended. The vulnerability of the Sonnets lies in their ceaselessly resistant reflection of this flaw, their stubborn reliance on economies incapable of correcting it, their use of language so wealthy, so charged with "difference," as to be erosive. The vulnerability of the Sonnets might be said to resemble that nameless flaw that afflicts their speaker, but in their case the flaw is not ultimately disastrous. They are not consumed by the extravagant husbandry that produced them. Their effort to resist, to compensate, to register in spite of slippage, balances their loss with store. They leave us with the awesome cost, and reward, of their conative contention. The vulnerability is inseparable from the striving that leads us to them: the "poet's" expense and Shakespeare's expense.

Toward a Poststructuralist Practice:
A Reading of Shakespeare's Sonnets

Howard Felperin

> *About anyone so great as Shakespeare, it is probable that we can never be right; and if we can never be right, it is better that we should from time to time change our way of being wrong.*
>
> T. S. ELIOT

I. EXEMPLARY TEXTS

Having argued that the institution of criticism should stop trying to do what it cannot do, i.e., seek out some monist or foundationalist rationale for its existence and activity—and continue to do what it can do, i.e., read and reread an ever negotiable canon of texts with all the resourcefulness available to it—I am duty-bound to set an example by putting that argument into practice. And since one of the resources currently available to criticism is that snowballing body of theoretical discussion which is the subject of this book, we can hardly do other than try its exegetical power by bringing it to bear upon a classic text. After all, if it has become a new institutional convention to theorize our practice, the least those of us can do who contest the pure good of theory from within it is to put to the test whatever value it holds for our practice, to read our canonical texts with one eye on them and the other on the theoretical journals. Or to put the matter the other way round, if one distinguishing feature of a classic text is its capacity, by virtue of the long interpretive tradition that has grown up around it, to read us even as we read it,

From *Beyond Deconstruction: The Uses and Abuses of Literary Theory.* ©1985 by Howard Felperin. Clarendon, 1985.

to register the pressmarks of our changing institutional discourse, then our classic texts should be able to tell us something about our theorizing, to refine it to a new level of self-consciousness, if not altogether out of existence.

No classic text illustrates this two-way traffic, or as we say now-adays, this intertextuality of our reading better than Shakespeare's Sonnets. In their unrivalled power to attract exemplary readers, the Sonnets have offered just such a window on criticism throughout their modern interpretive history. The richness of their rhetorical texture, loaded as it is with irony, paradox, and especially ambiguity, has provided grist for the processing—or overprocessing—of new-critical formalism, as exemplified by William Empson's reading of Sonnet 94 ("They that have power to hurt") (*Some Versions of Pastoral*). Northrop Frye, operating from a "critical middle-distance" where texture gives place to structure, has mapped the contours of the Renaissance "topocosm" they archetypify and the conventions of the sonnet they extend and culminate ("How True a Twain," in *Fables of Identity*). More recently, one of their number has been co-opted to fill out the paradigm of the structuralist analysis of poetic language developed by Roman Jakobson and Claude Lévi-Strauss. Has any of the poems chosen over the years by Jakobson for linguistic analysis demonstrated better than Sonnet 129 how poetic language is characterized by "the projection of the principle of equiv-alence from the axis of selection onto the axis of combination," or the "introverted nature of the poetic function," its concentration upon a "message," in which "everything becomes *significatif, récip-roque, converse, correspondant,* and . . . a perpetual interplay of sound and meaning establishes an analogy between the two facets, a rela-tionship either paranomastic and anagrammatic, or figurative (occa-sionally onomatopoeic)"?

I cite these readings of the Sonnets from among many others of the recent past, for the clarity with which they reveal the crystalline structure of the critical prisms that refract them. And as criticism now turns from its long preoccupation with such positive features of poetic language as form and genre, is there any text, or group of texts, in the literary canon that so readily lends itself to exploration of the negativities, absences, and indeterminacies of textuality itself? More specifically, is there any premodern text better suited to serve as a test-case for the universalizing claims of deconstruction, as a general theory of poetic or literary language (albeit a negative one) that has so far confined its hermeneutic practice largely to post-romantic literature? For despite the vast body of positivist scholar-ship on the Sonnets, with its restless reaching in a spirit of *Literatur-wissenschaft* after the biographical and historical identifications that supposedly explain them—in fact, as an unintended consequence of all that busy and contradictory scholarship—the Sonnets might well seem on the face of it to have been constructed, Shakespeare's pro-phetic soul dreaming on things to come, with the idea of deconstruc-tion in mind.

Consider their most obvious features as poetic narrative, fea-tures that remain striking and tantalizing in their undecidability or overdetermination in spite of all the scholarship they have occa-sioned. The Sonnets present to us a cast of characters—an ageing poet, a fair and noble youth, a successful rival poet, an untrustwor-thy dark lady—characters whose density and definition fluctuate un-predictably as the sequence progresses between the mimetic modes of allegorical abstraction and autobiographical concreteness. These characters make fitful appearances in a more or less triangular action as variously vivid and shadowy as their own characterizations. We hear of absences, betrayals, recriminations, and reconciliations coun-terpointed against the poet's continuing and self-conscious preoccu-pation with his art. We hear enough to persuade us that actual people and events in Shakespeare's life are here implicated, enough even to tempt us to try and reconstruct the intimate relations of the *ronde,* some acquaintance with which was presumably shared by that group among whom Shakespeare's "sugared sonnets" were circulating in manuscript by 1598. But what we hear is too little or too ambiguous to identify the players in this *drame à clef* with any assurance, or to interpret in detail the action it spasmodically advances, so much of its apparent burden of reference remains obscured between the poems and between the lines of the poems. Who, for example, had the power to hurt and did not use it?

But the invitation to a deconstructive rereading of the Sonnets proceeds from a congeniality anterior to the inbuilt discontinuities of the genre or the failure of an older historical scholarship to reach consensus on how to fill their gaps by identifying their protagonists and construing the relations among them. It arises rather from the peculiar nature of Shakespeare's Sonnets, as distinct from Sidney's or Spenser's, as a text that calls attention to its own literal textuality, its teasing and frustrating mode of existence as a printed book remote, distinct, orphaned from whatever authorial intentions, biographical retentions, and mimetic pretensions it might have been expected, in the light of conventional practice, to carry. The title page of the 1609 quarto bears no acronymic sublimations, unlike most Elizabethan sequences, of its protagonists or theme, merely the cryptic glorification of its "onlie begetter." The absent presence of this dedicatee has tempted and frustrated identification with the fair youth of the sequence, among a host of other candidates. Moreover, certain bibliographical and textual anomalies have led scholars, despite the fact that the poems are on the whole well printed, to propose numerous reorderings of the sequence to force its supposed plot to yield up its secrets. Yet after all these attempts at identification and rearrangement, only A. L. Rowse has arrived at confidence, a scholarly consensus of one. The positivist yearnings of an older historical scholarship to pin down the personal experience of an originary author are thus bound up with the dream of reconstructing a stable, authoritative text of the Sonnets. Both projects were baffled from the outset by the uncooperative aloofness of their freestanding textual autonomy.

Given the positivist incapability of an older biographical and bibliographical scholarship to fill the gaps in its own construction of the Sonnets, what followed was not a new negative capability in subsequent dealings with them. For such a labour of the negative was not always, and certainly not yet, thinkable in our institutional discourse. What followed was rather the displaced positivism of the new-critical and proto-structuralist analyses already mentioned, content to make due with the text as it stands but not quite content to relinquish the quest for unified and ascertainable meaning. For Northrop Frye, such problems as what actual people and events in Shakespeare's life his sonnets record, or whether the love professed in the earlier half of the sequence is homosexual were effectively dissolved, if never quite resolved, when the poems were regarded as expressions of a distinctively literary language. To the vexed question of whether some of the sonnets celebrate homosexual love, for example, Frye advances a uniquely modern answer: it doesn't matter. When read in terms of the conventions of Elizabethan sonneteering, within which mistresses are invariably female and fair, Shakespeare's sonnets offer no less than two masterly variations, two unprecedented moves in the game, by introducing two presiding mistress-muses, a "lovely boy" and "a woman coloured ill." They have less to say, that is, about "experience," particularly Shakespeare's own, than about poetry and its conventional and archetypical, ever-ready and ever-recyclable subject-matter. We find in the Sonnets, "the authority of Shakespeare behind the conception of poetry as a marriage of Eros and Psyche, an identity of a genius that outlives time and a soul that feeds on death." In his elegant appropriation of the leading motifs of the Sonnets, Frye redefines the source of their power over generations of readers as their paradoxically authorless authority, their equipoise between personal attitude and impersonal structure, their oscillation, as it were, between voice, with its individual "grain," and language or discourse, with its homogenizing conventionality. "The authority of Shakespeare," which Frye uncompromisingly refuses to locate in the biographical experience of the poet is none the less finally invoked in the more disembodied form of a reconstituted poetic tradition. A similar process of reestablishing the authority of the Sonnets on the basis, not of Shakespeare's supposed possession of his experience, but of his relation to his language, is at work in different ways in the notable studies of Sigurd Burckhardt and Roman Jakobson.

Yet such formalist or structuralist readings of the Sonnets, while they may foreclose certain traditional problems of interpretation, also create new ones. Is it sufficient any longer to locate the poetic authority of the Sonnets, their claim to being read as something like a type or definition of poetry itself, in Shakespeare's mastery of his literary or linguistic resources as distinct from the possession of his personal experience? Even if it were possible to do so at a time when the very existence of a distinctive and privileged poetic language is in question, would not the nature and conditions of such mastery have to be specified rather than merely assumed or asserted? The notion of authority seems to be inseparable from the notion of a personal author, of a literary will-to-power, yet the notions of genre, tradition, and language are all im- or trans-personal, and a *persona* is not a person. Thus Michel Foucault, addressing the question of authorship and echoing Roland Barthes's structuralist manifesto that "it is about time that criticism and philosophy acknowledged the disappearance or the death of the author," goes on to wonder "if this notion [of writing as having 'freed itself of the theme of expression,' as referring 'only to itself,' as 'opening up a space where the subject continually disappears'] does not transpose the empirical character of the author into a transcendental anonymity?" "Does not the representation of writing as an absence," he goes on, "simply repeat in transcendental terms the religious principle that tradition is at once unalterable and never complete, and the aesthetic principle of the survival of the work, its endurance despite death?" In illustration of the lingering inadequacy of the postmodernist deconstruction of authorship, Foucault asks: "If I discover that Shakespeare was not born in the house which one visits today, this obviously is not going to alter the function of the author's name; but if someone proves that Shakespeare did not write the sonnets which pass as his, that is a change of another kind, one that affects the function of the author's name," ("What is an Author?," *Partisan Review* 42, no. 4 (1975): 603–14). And in the latter hypothetical case, it need hardly be added, the way we would read the Sonnets, our sense of a distinctive will—pun intended—to expression (whatever may be expressed) and design on our response (however various that may be) at work within the linguistic machinery of the text. Neither the structuralist displacement of authorship into the transcendent authority of linguistic system, or of genre and tradition, nor the poststructuralist disappearance of the author into the transcendent anonymity of differential textuality seems quite able to obliterate our doubtless naive, superstitious, and romantic sense of the poet, in Wordsworth's words, as "a man speaking to men."

This rehabilitation of the residual subject, of the ghost in the machine of language, is already implicit not only in the contextualist poststructuralism of Foucault, but in textualist poststructuralism as well. For like Foucault, Paul de Man is sceptical of the capacity of structuralist and poststructuralist analysis of writing ever to do away with the need for an authorial subject, and expresses this scepticism in terms of the ancient—some would say anachronistic—concept of "voice":

> But even if we free ourselves of all false questions of intent and rightfully reduce the narrator to the status of a mere grammatical pronoun, without which the narrative could not come into being, this subject remains endowed with a function that is not grammatical but rhetorical, in that it gives voice, so to speak, to a grammatical syntagm. The term *voice,* even when used in a grammatical terminology as when we speak of the passive or interrogative voice, is, of course, a metaphor inferring by analogy the intent of the subject from the structure of the predicate.
>
> (*Allegories of Reading*)

The proscription of the intentional fallacy, devised by new criticism to rule out the too easy confusion of the literary and the empirical or biographical aspects of authorship, turns out to be very difficult to enforce. When it is strictly enforced, the authorial voice as will-to-expression is either transcendentalized into the authority of literary tradition itself, as in Frye's reading, or trivialized into the mechanistic anonymity of grammatical and linguistic forms, as in Jakobson's. From the poststructuralist perspectives of Foucault and de Man, the former operation delivers up a presence that, like godhead, is not really a presence but merely a resting-point for readerly anxiety in quest of presence (since the supposedly authoritative presence of literary tradition is constituted only by so many authors each as individually absent as the one in question); and the latter operation, an absence that is not really an absence, in so far as the apparently anonymous impersonality of linguistic manipulations, as in programmed computation, always implies someone, an intentional if not biographical subject, doing the manipulating.

Each of these poststructuralist reflections, different as they are in their contextual and textual emphases, reintroduces into the discussion of poetic authority an element that was notoriously absent from the diversely structuralist readings of Frye and Jakobson; namely, the historical and rhetorical dimensions, which are not simply assimilable to tradition or language. For Foucault, the idea of the author remains a meaningful but not metaphysical concept, a "strong moment of individualization in the history of ideas" and "a founder of discursivity." For de Man, literary or poetic language consists precisely in its rhetorical elusiveness, in its irreducibility either to the personal presence associated with voice or the impersonal constructions of language. What remains to be seen is how far these formulations can help to define the peremptory authority of Shakespeare's Sonnets over generations of readers, their special power as mighty begetters of readings. In what does that poetic authority consist, and by what is it conditioned? What is the nature of their Shakespearean rhetoricity and their Elizabethan discursivity, and what is the relation of the two?

II. Poetic Monuments

Obviously these questions can be engaged only through another reading of the Sonnets, one that would take account not only of their declared rhetorical ambitions, but of the undeclared discursive formations that condition them. In the interest of economy, we might do well to focus initially on a single sonnet, one that raises explicitly the question of poetic authority. Such sonnets are of course not hard to find in Shakespeare's sequence, and I have settled on Sonnet 55 for my point of departure. As one of the poetic "highs" of the Sonnets, asserting as it does in the most unequivocal terms its power to confer a special status on its author, its object, and itself, Sonnet 55 has always attracted critical attention. It has also been quite recently discussed as deriving directly from a sonnet by Spenser published in *The Ruines of Rome* (1591), itself a translation of one of Joachim du Bellay's *Antiquitez de Rome*. So Sonnet 55 plunges us, conveniently for our purposes, into that nexus of Renaissance intertextuality which might be termed the "ruins poem," contemporary examples of which occur in at least three European languages. Let us confine ourselves, however, to Spenser and Shakespeare:

> Hope ye my verses that posterity
> Of age ensuing shall you ever read?
> Hope ye that ever immortality
> So mean harp's work may challenge for her meed?
>   If under heaven any endurance were,
> These moniments, which not in paper writ?
> But in porphyr and marble do appear,
> Might well have hoped to have obtained it.
>   Nath'les my lute, whom Phoebus deigned to give,
> Cease not to sound these olde antiquities:
> For if that time doo let thy glorie live,
> Well maist thou boast, how ever base thou bee,
> That thou art first, which of thy Nation song
> Th'olde honour of the' people gowned long.
>
> (The Ruines of Rome, Sonnet 32)

> Not marble nor the gilded monuments
> Of princes shall outlive this pow'rful rhyme,
> But you shall shine more bright in these contents
> Than unswept stone, besmeared with sluttish time.
>   When wasteful war shall statues overturn,
> And broils root out the work of masonry
> Nor Mars his sword nor war's quick fire shall burn
> The living record of your memory.
>   'Gainst death and all oblivious enmity
> Shall you pace forth; your praise shall still find room

Even in the eyes of all posterity
That wear this world out to the ending doom.
    So, till the judgment that yourself arise,
    You live in this, and dwell in lovers' eyes.

Whether Spenser's sonnet is a "source" for, or "influence" on, Shakespeare's, and what such terms might mean within such a context of Renaissance intertextuality, are not of immediate concern. For our present purposes, it suffices that the two sonnets share a number of topics, tropes, and terms, and taken together, form a kind of meditation on Renaissance authorship. We may think of the relation between them as antiphonal or dialectical, whereby Spenser's sonnet frames, in the most tentative, even querulous, terms, a question to which Shakespeare's offers a supremely self-confident answer.

That question is not merely the literary one of how poetic authority, and the immortality consequent upon it, is to be achieved in contemporary practice, but the literary-historical one of what conditions and underwrites it. How, in a belated age and barbarous Northern vernacular, can the classics of insolent Greece and haughty Rome be equalled or surpassed? For both poems take as their point of departure the ringing claims of Horace and Ovid to a poetic survival beyond physical death and material decay, the word "monument," common to both sonnets, explicitly echoing Horace's "*exegi monumentum aere perennius.*" Both Horace and Ovid had based their poetic claims on Rome's imperial domination, and the insurance it provided for the universal literary hegemony of Latin. The problem facing the sixteenth-century English or French poet, as the Spenser/du Bellay sonnet makes painfully explicit, is whether a poem written in a belated vernacular can also aspire to immortality when it is not underwritten by the guarantee of imperial greatness, particularly when the very monuments that bear witness to Rome's and Egypt's grandeur have themselves crumbled. In projecting, tentatively in Spenser and confidently in Shakespeare, the power of poetry to transcend the power of empire, both poems are precursors of Shelley's "Ozymandias." While they hold no hint of the latter's romantic irony toward the aspirations of imperial conquest itself, both Spenser/du Bellay and Shakespeare anticipate something of Shelley's scepticism towards the imperial self-projections of monumental sculpture that go with it. So much so in Shakespeare's case, as to elaborate in terms even more explicit and extravagant than Horace's, the paradox that poetry, at least his own, will outlast—despite the apparent perishability of its graphic or vocal medium—the monumental art and architecture of royal conquest—despite the apparent durability of their harder media of marble and stone.

On what, then, is Shakespeare's poetic self-confidence grounded, if not on something like the imperial theme of his Roman precursors? Had Shakespeare taken a more Shelleyan approach to the Ozymandian situation he sketches, his confidence might well have been underwritten by a Neoplatonic poetic, certainly available to an Elizabethan poet and often invoked by Spenser, that asserts the eternality of spiritual form over its mutable material embodiments, and hence the superior potential of poetry as "airy nothing" to body forth "the forms of things unknown" over those plastic arts which still participate in the corruption of matter. Though Shakespeare might have appealed to Neoplatonic poetics, explicitly or implicitly, to support his claims, and seems to do so elsewhere, he does not do so in Sonnet 55. Given the extravagance of those claims, in fact, such an appeal would not really have lent much support. For even if poetry, by virtue of its linguistic medium, can be considered less material than the plastic arts, and hence suitable for the representation of a transcendent ideal of beauty, nobility, glory, or whatever, its claim to transcendence is still only relative, since manuscript, printed pages, and even the articulated breath of speech are still matter, and therefore subject to expiration and decay. But Shakespeare's claim, like Horace's and Ovid's, but unlike Spenser/du Bellay's, is absolute. It is made without Neoplatonic support, in defiance of conventional logic, and against historical precedent. After all, even if Shakespeare could not know of the fire in the Cotton library that was to decimate much of his own earlier national literature in 1731, he could not have failed to know of the calamitous burning of the Alexandrian library in 47 B.C., which consumed many a deathless classic among the forty thousand manuscripts destroyed.

Nor does Shakespeare's sonnet open an appeal, as several of his plays do, to any realist, as distinct from idealist, mimetic programme in staking its claim to poetic perdurability. The object that the poem promises to deliver up for all time is notoriously obscure. It is hard to say just what "these contents" even refer to, that are supposed to "shine bright." The youth's beauty? His nobility or achievements? His corpse? For the context of marble and stone monuments, the constricting form of the sonnet, and the closing anticipations of resurrection and judgement have suggested this last reference to some readers. We cannot even be sure that the "you" the poem addresses itself to representing is the youth. Northrop Frye registers Shakespeare's cavalier unconcern with exactitude or verisimilitude of reference and representation when he notes, with throwaway wit, that "although the poet promises the youth immortality, and clearly has the power to confer it, he does not lift a metrical foot to make the youth a credible or interesting person." The power of immortality which Shakespeare ascribes to his rhyme, and which his readers, with Frye, freely concede to him, does not seem to be based on or sustained by any a priori relation, any close or detailed resemblance, explicit or implicit, between poetry and material or empirical reality whatever. The claim of power is based on nothing other than its own assertion of power. It is entirely tautological, self-referential, and rhetorical. The power of poetic survival seems to consist solely in the poem's presumed rhetorical power to compel future readings: "As long as men can breathe, and eyes can see," Shakespeare writes in an analogous vein in Sonnet 18, "So long lives this, and this gives life to thee." Perhaps what is most remarkable about the claim is that it has proved to be entirely self-fulfilling.

In pointing to the rhetorical nature of Shakespeare's enunciation of poetic authority and perdurability in Sonnet 55, I am not suggesting that its force can be wholly explained in terms of a Renaissance rhetorical programme then in place, or that adherence to such a programme is what insures its poetic success. In fact, Shakespeare's poem, with its initial restatement and subsequent elaboration of a Horatian and Ovidian *topos,* does illustrate a principle fundamental to Renaissance rhetorical theory, namely that of *copia,* of virtuoso elaboration on a received theme. This widespread rhetorical practice may well be regarded as the Renaissance counterpart or forerunner of the post-romantic phenomenon of creative misprision, a means of engaging and overgoing classical models and thereby extending a potentially tongue-tying tradition by reweaving it.

Such commonplace rhetorical tactics as hyperbole and negative comparison, both employed in the opening line of Sonnet 55, are in the service of this larger rhetorical strategy. The frequent and characteristic recourse to hyperbole, often combined with classical allusion, is familiar enough as a chief constituent of Marlowe's mighty line, from which Shakespeare doubtless learned much, and negative comparison is one of the chief means by which Milton aspires to overgo classical epic, "to soar above th'Aonian mount": "*Not* that fair field of Enna." The extravagant variation on a received topic characterizes Shakespeare's own earliest efforts in epyllion, comedy, and tragedy; his *Venus and Adonis* and *Rape of Lucrece* multiply the metamorphoses of their Ovidian sources, and his *Comedy of Errors* and *Titus Andronicus,* the mistaken identities and vindictive atrocities of Plautus's *Menaechmi* and Seneca's *Thyestes* respectively. This rhetorical gambit is no doubt also at work in the bold paradoxes with which he develops the traditional poetic claims of Horatian and Ovidian sources in Sonnet 55, so as to revivify and redouble their old force through the surcharge of a new rhetorical *energia.*

It would be grossly reductive, however, to think that Sonnet 55—or the Sonnets generally, since this is their persistent under-theme—authorize themselves simply through the single-minded following out of a Renaissance rhetorical programme. After all, the strategy of *copia,* with its panoply of particular rhetorical tactics, is itself only a norm or model that by its own logic would itself have to be exceeded for a true authority to emerge. Great numbers of Elizabethan sonnets, including that of Spenser/du Bellay, make some of the same moves as Shakespeare's Sonnet 55 in rhetorically invoking and extending classical precedent to legitimate themselves, yet fail to make good their poetic aspirations in the only way they can be made good: by compelling future readings. Shakespeare himself complains halfway through his sequence that the imitation of his own rhetoric by rival poets has left him barren and tongue-tied, "enforced to seek anew / Some fresher stamp of the time-bett'ring days" (82.7–8). To achieve the kind of poetic authority Shakespeare envisions, he would have to tap some "source" deeper and more powerful than any set of classic examples or programme of rhetorical variation, thereby anticipating and preempting his own potential imitation and obsolescence at the hands of others. His poetry would have to be different from its own potential rhetorical reduction or anatomization.

This does not mean that the authority Shakespeare envisions and claims has nothing to do with rhetoric, only that it is not rhetorical in any simple sense, i.e., that it is not logical, or has empirical designs on its putative object and potential readers, or uses a repertory of devices for effecting those designs. The project so confidently proclaimed in Sonnet 55 seems closer to the rhetorical mode described by Paul de Man and Roland Barthes, as "performative."

Barthes defines a "performative" utterance, adopting the term from J. L. Austin, as "a rare verbal form (exclusively given in the first person and in the present tense) in which the enunciation has no other content (contains no other proposition) than the act by which it is uttered—something like the *I declare* of kings or the *I sing* of very ancient poets" ("The Death of the Author," in *Image-Music-Text*).

Though not exactly cast in present tense, and without giving up all empirical designs on its object and audience, Sonnet 55 seems very close to this performative mode in its aspiration to a royal or bardic bringing into being of its object, to making itself good and itself flesh in something like the eternal present of its utterance. So it might well seem tempting at this point to try to account for the triumphant poetic authority of Sonnet 55—as opposed to the more limited authority of any number of its Elizabethan congeners—as a function of this performative quality, that is, in terms of the consistency and integrity with which it maintains the self-subsistence of its performative mode. Such an approach would at least have the advantage of reinscribing the poem within the modernist, post-authorial, performative poetic advanced by Barthes, among others, within which "*writing* can no longer designate an operation of recording, notation, representation, "depiction" (as the Classics would say) and every text is eternally written *here* and *now*."

But there are some obvious difficulties in the way of such an approach. One is that it begs the question of value-judgement. The success or failure of performative utterance, like any other poetic mode, doubtless has something to do with its quality in the evaluative sense. Shakespeare, in fact, implies as much, that the immortality of his poem depends on just such a historical judgement, when he alludes to the Christian judgement that will ultimately determine the fate of the youth himself. It is only such a saving judgement of quality, after all, that could persuade posterity to take the necessary pains to preserve the paper on which his sonnets are written or printed—the paper we are repeatedly reminded, in this sonnet and elsewhere, is as subject to combustion, oxidation, and decay as "yellow leaves" themselves—in order to read and reread them in times to come, to give them breath and voice, and hence, their own "life" or "afterlife" by analogy with that of the youth they represent.

Here another difficulty emerges. For what conditions this necessary value-judgement is not intrinsic to the performative modality of its utterance. That in itself cannot make a poem good. If it could, or if Shakespeare and his fellow Elizabethans believed it could, such poet-kings as Marlowe's Edward II, Shakespeare's Richard II, and Ford's Perkin Warbeck, all of whom are magisterial exemplars of performative utterance, would have had to meet different, and better, destinies within their plays. Yet in none of these cases does their performance as poets ensure their historical success. Quite the opposite: their performative rhetoric, brilliant as it is, *fails* to carry the day. The value placed on performative utterance as such, whatever its technical or "intrinsic" quality, seems to be a function rather than a determinant of historical and cultural circumstance—as the outcome of each of these plays demonstrates, and Barthes's own highly polemical advocacy of it as the preferred modernist or postmodernist mode, itself attests.

But there is another, more formidable obstacle to identifying the claim of Sonnet 55 to poetic perdurability with its performative status as intransitive or apodictic writing, in Barthes's term, "inscription." Far from abandoning the notions of "recording, notation, representation, "depiction" (as the Classics would say)" in favour of present, personal, and noninstrumental "inscription," Shakespeare's Sonnets generally, and Sonnet 55 particularly, insistently press their mimetic and empirical claims, their designs upon a prior, nonlinguistic "reality" in order to fix and perpetuate it. How could it be otherwise, when Renaissance poetics is invariably mimetic in nature, and seems to know no other way in which to think of itself, to theorize its practice? In contrast to Barthes's "modern scriptor," for whom the intransitive autonomy of writing is to be welcomed with a sense of relief at least, of pleasure or joy at most, the Shakespeare of the Sonnets, particularly of the first half of the sequence, consistently regards his writing transitively, as deriving whatever freestanding autonomy it may achieve from the imitation, albeit heightened and hypertrophied, of an original in the way that Sonnet 55 projects. Very like a monument indeed. This is not to suggest that Shakespeare cannot imagine the mimetic failure of his art, the defectiveness or breakdown of his poetry as representation. He does so often in the sequence. But when he does so, the inadequacy of writing is always measured against a presupposed mimetic norm or ideal.

In the earlier phase of the sequence, especially in the first seventeen sonnets known as the "procreation series," the priority of nature to art, of the natural to the artistic project, is consistently asserted, and the role of poetry and the poet is conceived as unabash-edly empirical or instrumental, to persuade the youth to replicate himself by marrying and begetting children: "But wherefore do you not a mightier way / Make war upon this bloody tyrant Time?" (16.1–2). Poetry, however relentlessly mimetic, is seen as inferior and subservient—a mere "barren rhyme"—to the reproduction of nature itself, which is supposedly "Much liker than your painted counter-feit" (16.8), an invidious comparison carried to its self-denigrating and self-denying conclusion in the last of the procreation series, where the poet asks "Who will believe my verse in time to come?" and finally repudiates that verse on the grounds of its mimetic inap-titude: "It is but as a tomb / which hides your life, and shows not half your parts" (17.3–4). Even in the famous Sonnet 18 ("Shall I compare thee to a summer's day"), with which the poet's own wooing of the youth seems to begin in earnest, his "eternal lines" develop their newfound strength in representing their object of de-sire through a series of comparisons in which natural analogues now prove defective and invidious. The original inadequacy of mimesis has been more than made up in what can only be termed a supermi-mesis that actually replaces its object with a poetic counterpart ca-pable of withstanding all the destructive elements enumerated in the bold paradoxes of Sonnet 55.

But the abandonment of the initial empirical project of the Son-nets as persuasion to love, with its justification in a natural, material, and heterosexual reproduction of its object (in all its imperfection and perishability) in favour of the more idealized mimetic or super-mimetic project of a transcendent or transmaterial sublimation of or substitution for it, which culminates in Sonnet 55, turns out to be a pyrrhic and short-lived victory. This emerging repudiation of the supermimetic ambition to substitute the poem for the object of de-sire initially expresses itself as moral revulsion at the narcissism it involves: "Sin of self love possesseth all mine eye / . . .'Tis thee, my-self, that for myself I praise, / Painting my age with beauty of thy days" (62.1,13–14). But it increasingly involves a new consciousness of mimetic embarrassment as well, of the inbuilt frustration of any poetic attempt to transcend the residual materiality of its own utter-ance. The breath in which it is spoken, or the paper on which it is literally written, is, as we have already seen, an inescapable subver-sion and ironic self-denial of the claim to transcendent and perdur-able supermimesis enunciated in Sonnet 55.

The sonnets on time that follow and culminate in Sonnet 65 make even more explicit the contradictions of the supermimetic project by granting Time his full tyrannical due over every nook and corner, every last vestige, of material reality:

> Like as the waves make towards the pebbled shore,
> So do our minutes hasten to their end,
>
> . . . .
> And time that gave doth now his gift confound.
> Time doth transfix the flourish set on youth,
> And delves the parallels in beauty's brow,
> Feeds on the rarities of nature's truth,
> And nothing stands but for his scythe to mow.
> > And yet to times in hope my verse shall stand,
> > Praising thy worth, despite his cruel hand.
> >   (Sonnet 60)

> Against my love shall be as I am now,
> With time's injurious hand crushed and o'erworn
> When hours have drained his blood and filled his brow
> With lines and wrinkles,
>
> . . . .
> For such a time do I now fortify
> Against confounding age's cruel knife,
> That he shall never cut from memory
> My sweet love's beauty, though my lover's life.
> > His beauty shall in these black lines be seen,
> > And they shall live, and he in them still green.
> >   (Sonnet 63)

> When I have seen by time's fell hand defaced
> The rich proud cost of outworn buried age,
> When sometimes lofty towers I see down razed,
> And brass eternal slave to mortal rage;
>
> . . . .
> When I have seen such interchange of state,
> Or state itself confounded to decay,
> Ruin hath taught me thus to ruminate,
> That time will come and take my love away.
> > This thought is as a death, which cannot choose
> > But weep to have that which it fears to lose.
> >   (Sonnet 64)

Since brass, nor stone, nor earth, nor boundless sea,
But sad mortality o'ersways their power,
How with this rage shall beauty hold a plea,
Whose action is no stronger than a flower?
O how shall summer's honey breath hold out
Against the wrackful siege of batt'ring days,
When rocks impregnable are not so stout,
Nor gates of steel so strong but time decays?
O fearful meditation; where, alack,
Shall time's best jewel from time's chest lie hid?
Or what strong hand can hold his swift foot back?
Or who his spoil or beauty can forbid?
   O none, unless this miracle have might
   That in black ink my love may still shine bright.

                               (Sonnet 65)

These great "ruins poems" that dominate the sonnets of the sixties in Shakespeare's sequence may be read as a dark postscript to the bright promise of Sonnet 55. If 55 triumphantly substitutes, by a masterly if narcissistic sleight of hand, its own transcendent textuality for its mimetic object, thereby defeating time, these sonnets envision Time as himself a master-artificer of self-consuming artifacts, a kind of action-sculptor or action-painter gone berserk. For Time's fine frenzy climaxes in that masterstroke of his "cruel hand" which is the self-destruction of his own great works; his "transfixing" (60.9) of "the flourish" he himself has "set on youth" means not permanence but murder, and would have to be countered by a "strong hand" indeed. The struggle for immortality is now cast as a poetomachia, in which Time himself is seen by Shakespeare as a powerful rival, with the outcome quite uncertain as to which will prove *il miglior fabbro*. The ringing Horatian diction of Sonnet 55 is still invoked, but the claim of a poetry written in black ink on yellowing paper to outlast time's own favoured media of brass and stone now requires the "might" of a "miracle" to make itself good. The poetic imperative of Sonnet 55, through which poetry immortalizes by fiat its object and itself, has become in Sonnet 65 a merely subjunctive "might."

III. SPEAKING PICTURES

In recalling attention to the unlikely nature of "black ink" as a medium of representation—"His beauty shall in these black lines be seen, / And they shall live, and he in them still green"—Shakespeare returns, and returns us, through this radical defamiliarization of his medium, to the questionable mimetic potential of writing in comparison to that of the plastic and visual arts. And as we witness Shakespeare wrestling with the full dubiety of that issue, might we not well wonder why he should want or need to do so? Why should Renaissance poetry and poetics be unable to think of themselves as anything other than mimetic, despite the difficulties, so explicitly raised and addressed by the Sonnets, in maintaining that claim? Were it not better done, as our postmodernist poetics has long since done, to abandon all claims or pretensions to a lifelike mimesis, and settle for a concept of writing as a productive or constitutive, rather than imitative, function, more in line with our more general and modern understanding of the intransitive productivity of signs and sign-systems? After all, even painting and sculpture, apparently so much better adapted to the imitation of an object, have often in this century seen fit to abandon their traditional mimetic function in order to develop their own constructivist and productivist, abstract and expressionist potential.

Such changes in the rationale of the arts, in the discourse that explains and legitimates their function, clearly have at least as much to do with the changing historical and cultural conditions within which the arts are produced as with intrinsic aesthetic issues within and between them. In the case of Elizabethan sonnet-sequences, the system of aristocratic patronage that traditionally supported their production may well remain, as we say nowadays, "inscribed" in the poems themselves as well as in the Elizabethan poetic theory that surrounds them, and may well help to account for the dubious mimetic ambition they often express in terms of an equally dubious comparison with the visual arts. Even at a point when the poet was turning—and Shakespeare's career coincides with this point—from the service of the aristocracy, as the source of patronage and authority in commissioning works of art designed to confirm and perpetuate its own present power, to the practice of an art which could maintain and authorize itself by the more independent means made possible by the printing of books, even at such a point, the measure of poetic success was still conceived as the ability to render up a presence, if no longer of the embodied and institutional authority of the culture, at least of the poetic object. The noble youth of Shakespeare's sequence, whether or not he can be identified with the

Henry Wriothesley, Earl of Southampton, whose actual patronage Shakespeare seems unsuccessfully to have sought, may be read as just such a sign of transition within the poet's affairs. The authority of Shakespeare's Sonnets is conceived from within the Sonnets as insep-arable from their ambition to represent and perpetuate the active presence of the youth himself, despite the sublimation of his social authority into his power to compel love and devotion, and despite the dubieties that this representation in so unlikely a medium as "black ink" entails.

   If these speculations are at all valid, it follows that Shakespeare's retention of mimesis as the source of his own poetic authority rein-scribes in a displaced and metaphoric form an older discourse of ar-tistic authority based quite literally in the artist's proximity to the historical and social—the Marxists would say "real"—sources of power. The classic rationale of mimesis under which poetry and painting were still associated—*ut pictura poesis*—must then be under-stood as a new self-justification or self-authorization in the adopted terms of the displaced or substitutive presence that is metaphor. The access and proximity to "real" power once enjoyed by the arts under the system of ecclesiastical and royal or aristocratic patronage—a metonymic or literal authority—is giving way in the late Renaissance to a recreation in linguistic and poetic terms of that older, now dis-placed, relation—a metaphoric or figurative authority. Poetic lan-guage, as a displaced presence seeking to maintain through similarity the place it once occupied through contiguity, to close the gap of its displacement from centrality, by becoming the self-authorizing ob-ject of its own representation, thus takes on a newer metaphoric and an older metonymic aspect, which are blurred together under the concept of mimesis. The metaphoric similarity of poetic language to its authorizing object now becomes an issue, takes on a new and special urgency, in a way it never did before when the authority of poetic language was based on its metonymic contiguity to a "real," i.e., socially legitimate and authoritative, object. This new urgency becomes all the more intense and troubled when the conventional comparison with painting, slower to emerge into the dubious and anxious freedom from patronage conferred on writing by the print-ing press, is invoked. The by now familiar questions, raised by Ro-man Jakobson and others, concerning the relations of contiguity and similarity, syntagm and paradigm, metonymy and metaphor, *within* language and poetic language, could not have been raised until prior questions concerning the contiguity and similarity *of* language and poetic language in relation to a preexisting reality had been raised. The relative claims to priority or authority of metaphor and metonymy *within* the functioning of poetic language, could not become an issue until poetic language had been separated from a reality with which it had formerly been identified, that is, until its own relation to "reality" was conceived as merely metaphoric or metonymic, as in some sense figurative. This seems to occur late in the development of a culture, and in the case of European culture the moment of that anterior rethinking was the Renaissance, and its major text, Shakespeare's Sonnets.

Nor is it accidental that this rethinking of the relation between language and "reality" is conducted, within Renaissance poetics and Shakespeare's poetry, in terms of a sustained comparison with the visual and plastic arts in particular. Those sister arts of visual representation, particularly in their monumental forms, still aristocratically commissioned in Shakespeare's culture, would have seemed on the face of it, to enjoy at least two advantages over writing, so it is not really surprising to find writing appropriating their terms and assimilating itself to them. Sculpture and painting are both historically contiguous to their objects, their "sources" of cultural authority and prestige. They are or were adjacent in time and space to the tyrant, prince, or aristocrat who commissioned and presumably sat for them, or whose remains they commemorate or even literaly contain, and with whose actual person they may be, at least for a time, compared.

Their function as a mnemonic device, as a bid for eternal presence, moreover, is not only a matter of historical contiguity, but of material similarity, since stone, brass, and paint have a natural affinity with the human flesh they can be contoured and coloured to resemble, and thereby recall while replacing. The most striking illustration of this double mimetic advantage of monumental sculpture occurs in *The Winter's Tale,* where the similarity of Julio Romano's statue to the "dead" Hermione—to which everyone present attests—is further reinforced by its contiguity to Hermione's supposedly look-alike daughter, Perdita (conceivably played by the same actress) at its unveiling. "Had he [Julio] eternity himself, and could put breath into his work," remarks one of the onlookers, "he would beguile nature of her custom, so perfectly is he her ape" (5.1.105–8).

The advantage of mimetic contiguity of course fades with time and is always compromised by the inescapable conventionality of art, but these qualifications only allow the conversion of one advantage into the other. Even at a later historical stage, when art no longer directly represents the aristocratic or bourgeois power that commissions it, as in Velázquez's *Las Meninas,* it contrives to exploit its inbuilt implication of presence. Rembrandt's long sequence of self-portraits gains much of their force from the assumption of mimetic contiguity, from the illusion they continue to induce, as self-portraits, of our being as close as his own mirror to the very presence of the painter and of our watching, like a fly on that mirror, the simultaneous progress of his ageing and process of its recording in a kind of ultimate objectification or anatomization of subjectivity. The Egyptian pharaohs, who used to efface the names inscribed on the tombs of their predecessors and substitute their own, could thereby, thanks to the high and accommodating stylization of Egyptian art, enforce the sense of mimetic similarity through sheer historical contiguity. Even in Shelley's "Ozymandias," despite its ironic denial of the Egyptian conqueror's boast of eternal omnipresence, the speaker none the less feels himself very much in the presence, if not of this particular pharaoh, of the generalized passions of tyranny itself, which yet survive.

Poetry, by contrast, can make no such claim on the basis of its written medium even to the displaced presence that historical contiguity and material similarity confer on sculpture and painting. For writing, unlike the plastic arts, has only an arbitrary and conventional relation to its mimetic referent. Its referential function depends on the constitutive power of a system of signs that have no natural, material, or historical relation of contiguity or similarity to what they signify, but only an arbitrary and conventional one. Poetic representation is thus far more indirect and mediated than iconic representation, in so far as its arbitrary and conventional system of verbal signs requires a more complex and displaced reconstitution or concretization of the represented object. Our initial decipherment of poetic language is always already belated, occurs at a temporal and spatial remove from its putative object, and issues in a concretization of that object that is itself inescapably subjective, a filling-out of the inbuilt and necessary indeterminacies of textuality that is always dependent on prior beliefs, assumptions, and ideologies that vary from reader to reader and are never fully specifiable.

For the contextual and communal norms that might determine our reading of texts are themselves texts that require a further, ultimately elusive, determination. Writing, by putting the original context of language into radical abeyance, renders its objects simultaneously overdetermined and underdetermined in any readerly concretization of it. As a second-order system of representation neither deployed nor deciphered in the presence of its object, writing begins and remains on the far side of its object, remote and alienated from it, while continuing to aspire, at least in classical and Renaissance accounts, to re-present it. All the major Elizabethan sonneteers—Sidney, Spenser, and Shakespeare—recognize within their sequences the manifold difficulties involved in representing an object conventionally or actually "fair" in so unlikely, estranged, and unverisimilar a medium as the "black ink" of writing, while continuing to pursue that mimetic ambition. Yet it is only Shakespeare, as we shall see, who apprehends the full difficulty of that project while attempting a fully modern and writerly solution to it, which is to say, a solution that recognizes it is not a solution.

Before considering Shakespeare's distinctive "solution" to the paradox of writerly representation, let us look first at Sidney's more conventional approach to it. For Sidney's defence of the power of poetic language to represent a sensory world from which it seems to have forever taken leave is cast in precisely the terms we have already seen Shakespeare put into question: its supposed difference from the "black ink" of writing in general, and its supposed affinity with the visual arts. Contrasting the poet's representation of "concrete universals" with the particulars of historiography and the precepts of philosophy, Sidney contends that

> he [the poet] giveth a perfect picture of it [the general precept] in some one by whom he presupposeth it was done. . . . *A perfect picture I say,* for he yieldeth to the powers of the mind an image of that whereof the philosophers bestoweth but a wordish description: *which doth neither strike, pierce, nor possess the sight of the soul so much as that other doth.*
>
> For as in outward things, to a man that had never seen an elephant or a rhinoceros, who should tell him most exquisitely all their shapes, colour, bigness, and particular marks, of a gorgeous palace the architecture, with declaring the full beauties might well make the hearer able to

repeat, as it were by rote, all he had heard, *yet should never satisfy his inward conceits with being witness to itself of a true lively knowledge:* but the same man as soon as he might see those beasts well painted, or the house well in model, should straightways grow, without need of any description, to a judicial comprehending of them: so no doubt the philosopher with his learned definition—be it of virtue, vices, matters of public policy or private government—replenisheth the memory with many infallible grounds of wisdom, which, notwithstanding, *lie dark before the imaginative and judging power, if they be not illuminated or figured forth by the speaking picture of Poesy.*

("An Apology for Poetry," in *Criticism: The Major Texts* [italics mine])

The language in which Sidney maintains the classic claim of poetry, as distinct from other modes of writing, to the status of pictorial representation, is strikingly similar to that of the most sanguine of the Sonnets. For both Sidney and the Shakespeare of Sonnet 55, poetry does not so much "speak" as "perform" its object. It is a "perfect picture" that bears "witness to itself of a true lively knowledge"; it "illuminates" or "figures forth" what lies "dark before the imaginative and judging power." How close we are to the proclaimed "power" of Sonnet 55 to make its object "shine bright" and "pace forth" in time to come! And once again, this enunciation of visual and sensory immediacy is made in spite of the abstraction and distanciation, also acknowledged, inherent in the "wordiness" of its written medium. The paradox with which we began has not so much been resolved by Sidney as restated.

But not "merely" restated, in so far as Sidney's own language is itself "performative," or at least "rhetorical." The agency Sidney invokes as enabling poetry to bring off the miracle of achieving a representative power equalling that of the visual arts, despite the abstract wordiness of the written medium it shares with philosophy, is also the one he employs, namely, rhetoric or figurative language, the forms of language that George Puttenham terms "Sensable, because they alter and affect the minde by alteration of sense," i.e., language that violates or disturbs the conventional and normal, and therefore by received cultural association, the *naturalized* relation of sign and signification. The very phrase with which Sidney concludes his account of poetry's superior power of imaging its object illustrates precisely the operation it describes. The phrase "speaking picture" is first and foremost a metaphor, albeit a metaphor that has lost, through its repetition as a commonplace, the root meaning that George Puttenham, Englishing the nomenclature of classical rhetoric, translates as the figure of "transport," by which the qualities of one thing are transferred to something similar yet distinctly different, in this case the human voice to a mute visual image. Or it might be classified within Puttenham's scheme under the more radical figure which follows and extends metaphor, that of catachresis or "abuse," in so far as it applies to painting a term "neither natural nor proper" to "the thing we would seeme to expresse," a term blatantly inappropriate. Or it could even fall under paradox, or "the wondrer," since it reports "of a thing that is marvelous," the suggestion of a wondrous or marvelous power of poetry as all but unmediated vision being the point of Sidney's account (*The Arte of English Poesie*). Other figures could also be nominated.

My point in drawing attention to the figurative nature of the Renaissance commonplace Sidney employs is precisely that it draws attention to itself; by virtue of its semantic context and emphatic position in it, it begins to exemplify or perform the marvelous function Sidney describes, as the phrase activates in the mind the image of a picture speaking. In so doing, it re-produces the very effect of wonder that Sidney has just claimed for poetic language generally as an invisibly visual mimesis present to the mind's eye. Through Sidney's resurrection of a buried metaphor to active life, his revelation of an unforeseen fit between sign and signification, words and the sensory world they describe, a minor miracle has been performed. This is precisely what occurs in the final scene of *The Winter's Tale*, where Leontes, fancying that the statue of Hermione actually breathes, exclaims in wonder: "What fine chisel / Could ever yet cut breath?" (5.3,78–79). Shakespeare, a more excellent carver than either his own Julio or Paulina, has performed his own mimetic miracle in the line itself. Combining catachresis and onomatopoeia (Puttenham's "new-namer"), he has fixed our sense of wonder on a succession of monosyllables composed of short vowels chopped off by dental stops, and by so doing, has imitated in language the sharp clicks of a chisel tapping through its medium. What fine writing or speech could ever yet cut a chisel in the act of cutting? None other than Shakespeare's, and since it is nothing other than breath itself, i.e., the articulated air of dramatic speech, that is doing the cutting of breath, the art, as these Elizabethans would say, itself is nature, the word has performed its meaning.

IV. The Pun Made Flesh

The performative potential of rhetoric, it would seem, can begin to overcome, by altering the customary internal relations of language, its comparative disabilities in the foreign affairs of imitating a sensory world quite alien to it. The Sonnets of course offer countless examples of this kind of performative language, of what will later be termed "enactment," in which the normal linguistic relations between signifier and signified, sound and sense, form and meaning, are altered in what Puttenham terms "figures of disorder" as a way of opening an appeal from language to nature. Roman Jakobson has called attention to onomatopoeia as one of the chief poetic devices through which sound approximates sense, and it represents a classic example of the kind of language in which the differences between sign and referent that characterize language as a system are apparently foreclosed from the side of the phonetic signifier, much as they are by metaphor and its variants from the side of the semantic signified. (So much so, that Saussure felt the need to deal specifically with onomatopoeia as an apparent exception to the rule of arbitrary conventionality.) The textbook case of enactment for traditional poetics is Pope's example from Homer in his *Essay on Criticism*: "When Ajax strives some rock's vast weight to throw, / The line too labours and the words move slow." But the Sonnets offer more striking examples, such as the opening of Sonnet 129: "Th'expense of spirit in a waste of shame / Is lust in action." There, the sustained sibilance of air escaping past its labial and dental stops mimes the expenditure of vital "spirits"—the word held multiple Elizabethan meanings, from the physiological to the moral and theological—in the heavy breathing and piecemeal dying entailed in the sexual activity that this sonnet anatomizes.

Or consider another, related "auricular" figure, the one Puttenham terms "barbarism," since it depends on the phonetic unfamiliarity and consequent awkwardness of nonnative or incompletely naturalized, lexical material, such as we meet in the opening of Sonnet 116: "Let me not to the marriage of true minds / *Admit impediments.*" Here, the tongue-twistingly Latinate phrase "admit impediments" becomes itself an impediment, through its polysyllabic materiality, to the fluent nativism of the opening line, an obstruction placed in the way of Shakespeare's nimble feet (the word's etymology, in fact) and our tripping tongues, a material reminder that the course of true love can only run smooth through an act of will that transcends all obstacles. Or the recovery of that linguistic materiality which enables language to regain its mimetic affinity and aptitude may take advantage of its graphic, and thereby spatial, dimension. This also occurs in Sonnet 116: "Love's not time's fool, though rosy lips and cheeks / Within his bending sickle's compass *come*." The displacement of the verb "come" from its normal position in the middle to the end of the clause—the figure is "histeron proteron," termed by Puttenham "the preposterous"—defers comprehension of the line, our gathering or reaping of its sense, in a way mimetic of the action of the reaper's bending sickle, as it gathers to itself roses and youthful flesh at the end of their natural lives. The human life-span has been mimetically comprehended in Shakespeare's grammatical, i.e., graphic and spatial, dislocation of the conventions of his verbal medium.

Let us return, then, to Sonnet 55, in order to try out the skeleton key that the recuperative programme of Elizabethan rhetoric provides, and see whether it will unlock the secret of Shakespeare's claim to poetic and mimetic perdurability. If Roman Jakobson had analysed 55, one of the things he would have noticed in its first strophe is the high incidence of alliteration on "m," "p," and "s," which is repeated in the third strophe. That Shakespeare "affects the letter" in these strophes, and that they are thereby linked at the phonetic level is not in question. Our question is what performative relation this purely formal linkage at the level of the signifier might bear to the sonnet's signification, its "contents" as Shakespeare equivocally puts it. Here Jakobson can be of little help, taking as he notoriously does, meaning or content for granted or reducing it to the received ideas of other commentators. In the terms of his analysis, the most the empirical fact of alliteration can be is an earnest of poetic power, alerting us that some extra-communicative intention may be at work; in itself, it cannot be a source or explanation of that power. Occurring as it does within a semantic field that the alliteration does not itself generate, the function of alliteration cannot be causal or integral to signified meaning. Rather, it operates here as what Puttenham would call a figure of "ornament" of the kind Shakespeare designates and illustrates as such in the previous sonnet

("O how much more doth beauty beauteous seem / By that sweet ornament . . ."). As ornament or decoration, alliteration bears the same superficially attractive but functionally inessential relation to the poem as "gilt" does to the "monuments / Of princes" mentioned at the outset. Gilding is to monumental sculpture as alliteration is to the sonnet.

This analogy, if we allow it to guide our reading, would make the sonnet itself a monument or tomb containing the earthly remains of a prince or noble. Indeed, there is much to suggest, and nothing to deny, just such a reading. We have already seen that several of the Sonnets similar to 55 in form, theme, and diction explicitly compare themselves, as monuments to the beloved, triumphantly or unhappily to "tombs of brass" (10.7–14) and "a tomb / Which hides your life" (17.3–4). The editor of the latest, most intelligent edition of the Sonnets [Stephen Booth], glossing the phrase "in these contents," plausibly suggests that the "word *in* and the idea of the poem as a receptacle make the phrase ominously reminiscent of *monuments:* the phrase carries a suggestion of "in this coffin," a suggestion given scope by the vagueness and imprecision of *these contents* as a means of expressing "this poem" or "these lines." The suggestion gathers even greater force with the third and fourth strophes, in which the beloved object is said to "pace forth" and "still find room" by analogy with a Christian or Christological resurrection that transcends the confinement of the tomb.

This implicit depiction of the sonnet as a coffin or tomb, with the beloved as the body it contains, is an example of the figure Puttenham loosely terms "icon, or resemblance by portrait, and ymagerie." Even without an Elizabethan tradition of emblem poetry refined to a fine art by Donne and Herbert to encourage such resemblances, the four-square block of print the sonnet presents on the page would make it easily assimilable to the form of a box. Given this rough resemblance, Shakespeare's opening paraphrase of Horace works to carve it more finely into a verbal icon of the poem as mausoleum or sarcophagus. The economy of inflection lends Horace's Latin—*exegi monumentum aere perennius*—something of the epigrammatic concision of an epitaph such as might actually appear inscribed on the base of a monument or the lid of a sarcophagus, a pointedness that is of course much harder to attain in the uninflected volubility of English. Yet the syntactical structure of the opening line of Sonnet 55, and again of line 7, as well as the opening of 107 on the same theme—the "Not . . . nor" or "nor . . . nor" construction—may well represent Shakespeare's attempt to reproduce in English something like the epigrammatic symmetry of Latin by adopting and translating its classic "*nec . . . nec*" construction. This impression of latter-day Latinity may be further reinforced within the "nor . . . nor" clause of line 7 by the inclusion of a Latinate metonymy ("Nor Mars his sword"), whereby the name of the Roman war-god and its archaic genitive is paralleled with its modern English equivalent ("nor war's quick fire").

These Latinate usages suggest, particularly in the context of the Spenser/du Bellay sonnet quoted above, a kind of double resurrection at work. On the one hand, Shakespeare's pseudo-Latinity lends his sonnet something of the quality of an epitaph proclaiming the resurrection of the body contained within the mausoleum or sarcophagus of the sonnet itself. On the other, it performs a resurrection of the dead language of Latin poetry into the life of a modern European vernacular. The effect is analogous to that produced at the climax of *Julius Caesar,* a play dense with internal reference to monumental sculpture and carving, when Caesar breaks into Latin at the moment of death—"*et tu Brute*"—only to return to English, but an English cadence closely modelled in its dying fall upon that patch of Latin—"Then fall Caesar." The lapse into Latin and relapse into English dramatize the time-transcending claim made earlier by the play's co-carver of Caesar's fate, Cassius, that their bloody scene will be reenacted "in states unknown, and accents yet unborn" (3.1.113), a claim analogous to that of Sonnet 55, and one that similarly depends on the performative potential of the poetic medium to reproduce a "living record." "When you entombed in men's eyes shall lie," Shakespeare writes in Sonnet 81, "Your monument shall be my gentle verse / Which eyes not yet created shall o'er-read, / And tongues to be your being shall rehearse." In so far as the monumental statuary, mausoleums, and sarcophagi of the classical world have been mimed in the poetic form of the sonnet itself, as well as in some of its phonetic and syntactical units, the classical world has here been literally and fully textualized, rendered into a "speaking picture."

And if such a project of performative reappropriation is indeed at work in the poem, is it entirely fanciful to read the transition from its third quatrain—in which the beloved is envisioned as about to "pace forth" and "find room"—to its closing couplet—in which a last judgement of Christian resurrection is proleptically invoked—as enacting the change of state promised at the outset, the release of the beloved from imprisonment in the tomb of history into the liberty of textuality? Is it entirely fanciful to read the final couplet as a turning of the hinges of the poem, an unsealing of the tomb or swinging open of the coffin-lid through which the youth is released from the box of the sonnet's four-square quatrains in order to live and roam abroad, even increase and multiply, in the free, lively, and endless reflection of the "lovers' eyes" that will read the poem? Indeed, is this entire exercise in reading the sonnet, as a sustained attempt at hyperconcretization, at substantiating the claim of poetic language to equal mimetic power with the visual arts by recalling attention to poetry's own carving of its phonetic and graphic materiality, no more than an exercise in metaphor-making, a fallacy of imitative form, however seriously encouraged and underwritten it may be by Elizabethan poetics?

Before reaching that conclusion and dismissing the entire project of enactment, what Shakespeare himself terms "speaking in effect," as a kind of writerly pathetic fallacy, it is worth pointing out that the poetics of enactment are not a peculiarly Elizabethan superstition or caprice but seem to persist, in modified but still recognizable versions, into this century. The Russian formalists, for example, like the Elizabethans, see language as aboriginally poetic, and similarly identify its performative potential in the storehouse of metaphor that lies buried within it. Words, in the highly metaphoric words of Viktor Shklovksy, "complete the journey from poetry to prose," lose their visual and sensory value, their metaphoric density, through time and use, and wear away into thin and transparent counters of thought ("The Resurrection of the Word," in *Russian Formalism*). The poetic project then becomes "the resurrection of the word," its "rebarbarization" through such tactics as "defamiliarization," "retardation," "staircase-effect," and a general strategy of "baring the device." This heightening of technical consciousness is in the service of enabling us to see and hear again through poetic language what ordinary language has obscured and abstracted into mere recognition, much as people who live by the sea do not hear the waves, or a man does not notice the walls of his own room. How far is this, after all, from the claim of sensory presence advanced by Sidney and the Elizabethans?

Similarly with the poetics of F. R. Leavis, who independently advanced the criterion of enactment as the touchstone that distinguishes poetic authenticity. Leavis's enactive poetics takes the form of a series of practical value-judgements, whereby a poetry of sensuous concreteness, such as we find in Eliot, some of Keats, Blake, Pope, and Milton, but preeminently in Shakespeare, Donne, and the Metaphysicals carries the day against the abstraction of Shelley and most of Milton. It is through enactment, the term Leavis regularly employs, that the best poetry recovers for language an emotional and moral integrity with the "real" and "human" world that has been rendered increasingly precarious since the "dissociation of sensibility," of thought from feeling, that supposedly occurred during the seventeenth century. The synthetic, sensuous wit of metaphysical, as opposed to romantic, poetry becomes the model of poeticity itself in its attempt to recover a full mimetic presence and univocality, all but lost yet still recuperable. Like that of the Russian formalists, though without a thoroughgoing theoretical programme to support it, Leavis's poetics of enactment is a polemic in the service of a certain contemporary poetic practice that legitimates itself in a myth of lost linguistic origins, an essentially religious or sacramental or superstitious view of language as a bygone original presence now fallen into abstraction, alienation, and division. Once again we do not seem to be very far from Sidney, Puttenham, and the Elizabethans.

V. The Flesh Made Pun

Or perhaps more accurately, we seem to be so near and yet so far from them. So near, in the residual belief, superstitious or religious as it may be, that the poetic word once possessed and can still recuperate its lost integrity and univocality with the world, through some version of the enactive or performative process. And yet we are so far from the Elizabethans in that our post-Saussurian understanding of language, with its foregrounding, not to say fetishizing, of inbuilt structural difference and deferral—both that between signs themselves and that between the sign and any fully determinate meaning, let alone external reference—is so radically and unrecuperably *counter-enactive*. In the work of Shklovsky, for example, it is never fully clear whether the revivifying power ascribed to poetic language is directed toward reviving our perception of the world or merely of the word. The process of reinvesting language with its lost density by defamiliarizing it, and thereby concentrating our attention on it as language, cannot help but render it opaque, not more but less transparent upon or reflective of, a signified world. Our access to any prior, nonlinguistic reality that might exist is jeopardized, not enhanced, by that programme. The referential value of language must, as modernist poetics is well aware, decrease in proportion to its self-referentiality. It is the constitutive and generative, rather than the reflective or mimetic, power of poetic language, as Trotsky understood only too well, that Shklovsky and the formalists are asserting and giving new priority. Form, after all, generates content, and not *vice versa*.

For even if the supposedly aboriginal metaphoricity of language could be fully resurrected, its mimetic power would not be all that is recovered. Would it not carry with it a renewed sense of insuperable difference and duplicity, since metaphor is not natural magic but word-magic, not the recovery of hidden connection between words and world but continuing linguistic difference masquerading as identity? The persistent reinvestment of the poet with Orphic or Adamic powers of restoring to language a primal univocality is itself a rhetorical gesture. Similarly with Jakobson's model of language as communication, in which poetic language concentrates attention upon the message and its internal relations, thickens the medium, as it were, to the point where sender and receiver virtually drop out of the picture, as they in fact do in Jakobson's analyses of poetic texts. The paradox that haunts all performative accounts of poetic language, Elizabethan and modern, is that the means of recovering lost integrity and univocality is a further linguistic disturbance, a shattering of accustomed internal linguistic relations that can be recodified at a higher level but never reunified under any rhetorical programme, however elaborate. Rhetorical figuration, far from repairing the putative rift between sign and meaning, becomes only an encyclopedic record of the possibilities of this dislocation, which when applied in practice, only reenacts that dislocation. This paradoxical condition cannot be dialectically resolved from within the logic of an enactive poetics. Defect cannot be made up by more defect, by what Puttenham classifies as "figures of disorder" and "figures of default."

Or can it? Perhaps there is still some means available to language to repair its own defect as a mimetic medium, to enable it to achieve the legendary supermimesis of Apelles' Venus, invoked as analogy for Shakespeare's Cleopatra, which supposedly makes "defect perfection." It is just such an interrogation of the adequacy of any rhe-

torical programme to reproduce an object at all that lies at the core
of Shakespeare's sequence, the poems from 76 to 106, and that issues
in the partial solutions embodied in the figures of the rival poet and
ultimately of the dark lady herself. At this stage, the sequence turns
self-consciously metamimetic, questioning from within itself, even
to the point of "tongue-tied" silence, its own capacity, and that of
the rhetorical repertory generally—"What strained touches rhetoric
can lend" (82.10)—to represent the youth at all.

The problem is now conceived as twofold: not only is the
youth's beauty so transcendent as to strain to the limit the resources
of Shakespeare's own rhetoric, but the inadequacy of that rhetoric
has been revealed by its having been imitated and exceeded at the
hands of rival poets, "As every alien pen hath got my use / And
under thee their poetry disperse," (78.3–4). Let us leave aside for the
moment the punning allusion to literary patronage and sexual infidelity and confine ourselves to the rhetorical implications. A rhetoric
that derives its performative capability from its disturbance of conventional usage has itself become conventional usage, thereby re-
quiring a further disturbance to maintain its mimetic advantage. This
heightened awareness of rhetorical limitation is doubly difficult to
transcend, since what has been revealed to Shakespeare is at once
"How far a modern quill," despite the eager ingenuity displayed
around him, "doth come too short" (83.7) and the essential poverty
of his own rhetorical invention, its inability to overgo itself and
thereby overgo his imitators and rivals: "Why is my verse so barren
of new pride, / So far from variation and quick change?" (76.1–2).
In these sonnets, Shakespeare comes up against the paradox of a self-
superseding modernity: "Finding thy worth a limit past my praise, /
and therefore [am] enforced to seek anew / Some fresher stamp of
the time-bett'ring days" (82.5–8). If rhetoric, as Hopkins remarked,
"is the teachable part of poetry," then some new and unprecedented
rhetorical resource beyond the present state of the art, must continually be found.

Shakespeare meets this double dilemma with a two-pronged
strategy. On the one hand, he bequeaths to other poets "What
strained touches rhetoric can lend" (82.10), ascribing to them—
preeminently to that red herring of biographical research, the "rival
poet" (the dark lady being its Loch Ness monster)—an embodied
fullness of rhetorical powers he claims no longer to have himself, or
have any use for ("Was it the proud full sail of his great verse," 86.1),

and which in any case miss the mark of mimetic adequation, however effective they may be in seducing the youth. And on the other, he pursues a new self-conscious minimalism in his own writing, a wavering between plain speech and tongue-tied silence, which claims to hit the mark precisely because of its acknowledged inadequacy:

> This silence for my sin you did impute,
> Which shall be most my glory, being dumb;
> For I impair not beauty, being mute,
> When others would give life, and bring a tomb.
> There lives more life in one of your fair eyes
> Than both your poets can in praise devise.
>
> (Sonnet 83)

> Truth needs no colour with his colour fixed
> Beauty no pencil, beauty's truth to lay:
> But best is best, if never intermixed?
> Because he needs no praise, wilt thou be dumb?
> Excuse not silence so, for't lies in thee ‹the muse›,
> To make him much outlive a gilded tomb,
> And to be praised in ages yet to be.
>
> (Sonnet 101)

But this Neoplatonic or Keatsian approach—heard melodies are sweet, but those unheard are sweeter—has its own inbuilt poetic handicap, and as Shakespeare fully recognizes, a certain defeatist potential.

In setting up the rhetorical eloquence of the rival poet as a foil to his own more eloquent understatement, Shakespeare does not so much transcend the problem of rhetorical defect as defer it: "Where art thou, muse, that thou forget'st so long / To speak of that which gives thee all thy might?" (100.1–2). The ingenious solution of abjuring rhetoric and "speaking in effect"—"Then others for the breath of words respect, / Me for dumb thoughts, speaking in effect" (85.13–14)—turns out to be no solution at all, in so far as it is still speaking and still rhetoric, albeit a self-deprecating or self-denying rhetoric of understatement. What Shakespeare has done in this phase of the sequence is to exchange one rhetorical programme for another, a rhetoric of presence, fullness, immediacy, and enactment—now ascribed to and personified by the hypothetical rival poet—for a rhetoric of difference, deferral, indirection, and counter-enactment, involving a new set of dominant figures—those Puttenham terms "figures of default"—and generating a new set of thematic oppositions and contrasts—between himself and his rivals, poetry and its object, past and present poetry. The rationale for this new programme is that of *reculer pour mieux sauter,* that rhetorically less is mimetically more, as if a fault in the medium of representation can still be made fortunate. The earlier project of poetic fullness, of rivalling or replacing through a poetics of enactment the fullness of "great creating nature"—set out in the initial "procreation sequence"—a "second nature" that rivals and replaces the first, fallen one, has not so much been abandoned as reconceived.

It remains to be seen, however, whether this latest programme of "speaking in effect" can recuperate the enactive project, can make effective, let alone perfect, the "defect" in which it seems to be based, or whether its promise of enactive recuperation is haunted by linguistic bad faith from the beginning. For this latest turn in Shakespeare's search for a rhetoric of mimetic adequation, as the phase that names it suggests, seems to be rooted in nothing more than a pun. "Speaking in effect" can mean either "speaking effectively" or "speaking by default," or "defectively," i.e., "not speaking at all." We have already seen how, in Shakespeare's earlier and more straightforwardly enactive practice, so much depends on those figures which work to overcome conventional difference, to reinforce our sense of the shaky resemblance and relation between sign and signification, such figures as metaphor, catachresis, icon, and preeminently onomatopoeia, Puttenham's "new namer." Yet all of these devices, as they work locally to bring likeness out of conventional difference, also draw attention to themselves as devices, and thereby re-represent difference and deny resemblance. They act, as Puttenham might say, as "double agents" who betray the cause of enactment and play into the hands of its mighty opposite, a poetics of counter-enactment, nowadays known as deconstruction. The poetics of counter-enactment also has its master-trope, its chief figure, the very opposite of onomatopoeia, the "new-namer," and that figure is paranomasia, in Puttenham's scheme, "the nick-namer," or as it is better known to us, wordplay, pun, or quibble.

If the figures of enactment, of "speaking in effect" in Shakespeare's phrase, work cumulatively to integrate the jigsaw puzzle of language into a concrete replica of the sensory world, the pun is precisely that piece of language which will fit into several positions in the puzzle and thereby confound attempts to reconstruct the puzzle into a map or picture with any unique or privileged reliability or fidelity of reference. Whereas metaphor and onomatopoeia attempt to bridge the precipitate fissures between signs and their meanings, paranomasia effectively destabilizes further whatever conventional stability the relation between sign and meaning may be thought to possess. The pun is the concealed fault-line that reticulates the landscape of language, hardly visible until it slips, but once it does, the serene linguistic landscape is suddenly and totally transformed. Doubly anarchic, the pun can and often does collapse not only the horizontal differentiations in the outstretched panorama of signs that hold the system of language in place, but the hierarchical structures of "high" and "low" discourses or styles erected upon it as well.

Whereas metaphor tends to operate across discourses, while enforcing class distinctions within them, the pun is well suited to turning these vertical structures topsy-turvy, and hence, as Puttenham is well aware, especially useful for comic and carnivalizing effect. It brings low the conventionally high and upraises the conventionally low. It is no wonder, then, that the pun is proverbially regarded as the lowest form of wit, subversive as it is of second-order conventions of decorum, of the socially determined relations that are at once reflected and reinforced in daily linguistic usage, so that the laughter it provokes is often reluctant, uncertain, anxious, or disapproving. We are not always pleased to be reminded, as the pun reminds us, that the sociolinguistic house in which we dwell is not so well constructed as we might wish to think, that not only the individual bricks of which it is made, so firmly separated by mortar joints, but the floors on which we stand, may suddenly, handy-dandy, change places around us. At the very least, it reminds us of the arbitrariness of language as a system of differences, and at most of the conventionality of the social relations that system reflects and reinforces.

Now if Shakespeare is the poet whose power of metaphor and enactive language is generally acknowledged to be unsurpassed—a traditional view which my technical analysis of these effects so far only confirms—he is also the poet most notoriously given to the counter-enactive subversions of the pun. "A quibble was the golden apple," wrote Samuel Johnson, "for which he would always turn aside from his career, or stoop from his elevation," "the fatal Cleopatra for which he lost the world, and was content to lose it." The anxiety that speaks through Johnson's strictures doubtless arises from the threat posed by Shakespeare's wordplay to the "natural order" that any poetic classicism and social conservatism, however flexible, must presuppose. "Take but degree [i.e., hierarchical difference] away, untune that string," as Shakespeare's Ulysses puts it, "And hark what discord follows." If princes and gentlewomen can quibble indecorously with and like fools and clowns, even at moments of the highest passion and deepest pathos, then two "natural" orders are simultaneously threatened by this blurring of difference, one *by* language and the other *of* language.

The neoclassical social and moral ideals of sincerity and integrity, the virtues of the "honest soul," are simultaneously undermined as criteria of poetic value, since they depend on a reliable correspondence between sign and meaning. The destabilization and fragmentation of meaning effected by the pun, in which the material similarity or identity of two or more signs dissolves into two or more distinct and often antithetical meanings, can only reflect a disintegrated consciousness destructive of traditional moral and mimetic claims. Any attempt to read Sonnet 129, for example, as a moral tract against concupiscence, is defeated precisely by its puns, as such words as "spirit" (i.e., "sprit") and "heaven" (i.e., "haven") oscillate dizzily in Swiftian fashion between their abstract and concrete, sublime and ridiculous, religious and genital meanings. Similarly, any attempt to read it as philosophical poetry in the lofty, generalizing vein of *An Essay on Man* is undone by the puns of the final couplet on "well" ("will," and "Will" Shakespeare) on which the poem turns from impersonal pronouncement into a curiously resigned or bemused, even somewhat sordid, personal confession.

What with its demonumentalization of fixed or "natural" meaning, Shakespeare's wordplay would seem to be the ultimate "figure of disorder." From the viewpoint of an enactive poetics, it is counterproductive in the extreme, a denial and demystification of the lofty claims to poetic monumentality advanced in Sonnet 55. If anything, the pun seems to play into the hands of the enemies, Time and Death, not only in the structural sense that it undermines the monumental integrity of the word by fracturing its meaning and thereby "roots out the work of masonry," but also in the historical sense that the connotations it activates, particularly its lower ones, are often of a local or colloquial nature—as with the Elizabethan "sprit" ("erect phallus")—and therefore likely to be lost on posterity, while its root, etymological meanings are often already lost on all but the most historically and philologically erudite, as modern readers of Shakespeare's comedies will attest. The cult of etymology and etymological puns in the Renaissance as a favoured means of concentrating present meaning by recovering supposed origins can counterproductively turn the poet, as in the case of its foremost practitioner Spenser, into a poet's poet at best and a scholar's poet at worst—a destiny quite the opposite of the timeless and universal immediacy projected by an enactive poetics. Yet Shakespeare notoriously and unremittingly puts his enactive poetics at risk by cultivating the pun, and often the etymological pun.

There is no better example of a sonnet rooting out its own masonry, risking its monumentalizing immediacy, and counteracting its own enactment, than Sonnet 107, already cited as a companion piece to Sonnet 55 in its self-monumentalizing theme and its ringing "Not . . . nor" opening. Leaving aside the radical wordplay of "the mortal moon hath her eclipse endured," with its all but infinite variety of reference assiduously and unsatisfactorily explored by scholars—does the phrase not epitomize the restlessness of reference itself, the ebb and flow of phonetic and semantic flux?—let us proceed to the third quatrain, in which the triumph of writing over the historical mutability of time and death is asserted:

> Now with the drops of this most balmy time
> My love looks fresh, and death to me subscribes,
> Since spite of him I'll live in this poor rhyme,
> While he insults o'er dull and speechless tribes.
> And thou in this shalt find thy monument
> When tyrants' crests and tombs of brass are spent.

Though more provisionally than in Sonnet 55—for here the poem refers to itself as a "poor" rather than "powerful" rhyme, whose monumental status is no longer apodictic but remains to be found—the triumph over Time and Death is none the less proclaimed, and more remarkably still, it is proclaimed as having been wrought with their own weapons.

For the etymological puns on "subscribes" and "insults" revivify the old Latin senses of those words, which work here to reinforce their more modern and abstract meanings. Death "subscribes" to Shakespeare not only in the abstract sense of "submits" or "enters into agreement" but in the concrete, enactive sense of writing one's name at the bottom of a document, in this context a lease on life or peace treaty, and Death is forced to do so with the "drops" of Shakespeare's own ink! After such terms of surrender, the only victory remaining for Death is the hollow one over those hypothetical "speechless tribes," whom he will continue to "insult"—in the older sense of "leap against" or "assault" and in the later sense of "verbally abuse"—without any possible comeback. By reactivating through wordplay these decayed senses and pressing them into the service of his writing, Shakespeare imagines himself defeating Time and Death at their own war game, temporarily arresting the historical fluctuations of language that undermine masonry, and fixing these words permanently into place within his poetic monument.

It seems that even the most potent weapon of counter-enactment and destabilization, the pun, can be pressed into the service of poetic enactment and presence, and victory snatched from the jaws of devouring Time himself! Indeed, the very next sonnet ("What's in the brain that ink may character") self-consciously celebrates, through a series of writerly puns, just such an improbable victory:

> So that eternal love in love's fresh case
> Weighs not the dust and injury of age,
> Nor gives to necessary wrinkles place,
> But makes antiquity for ayc his page,
> Finding the first conceit of love there bred
> Where time and outward form would show it dead.
>
> (Sonnet 108)

If puns—and these lines contain several: on "case," "injury," "age," "antiquity," "aye," "page," "conceit," "would"—and particularly etymological puns, are the wrinkles carved by Time on the once clear face of meaning, what Shakespeare has done is to include the work of time within his own work in such a way as to arrest flux and preempt obsolescence. "Wrinkles" may be an organic necessity in the progress of nature toward death, but by giving them a place in his work he denies them priority or pride of place.

This was his practice, as far back as Sonnet 18—"Nor shall death brag thou wand'rest in his shade / When in eternal lines to time thou growest"—though here in Sonnet 108 it has become fully and self-consciously foregrounded. Lines of living become lines of verse; classical antiquity, the freshly written page; the tomb or coffin of the love-sonnet, the tome or show-case from which love rises afresh to the reading eye for aye. The most astute modern reader of the Sonnets [Stephen Booth] is surely—and quite uncharacteristically—under-reading this sonnet, when he demurs over earlier editor's paraphrasing of its closing strophes as a "continuation of the discussion of literary invention in lines 1–8," suggesting that it "exaggerates the purposefulness and continuity of *this secondary train of thought,*" (italics mine). Only by maintaining the priority of the sonnet's, indeed the sequence's, empirical or mimetic over its writerly and metamimetic enterprise could Booth relegate this train of thought to a "secondary" status.

Such a demurrer, coming as it does from a reader on whom few of Shakespeare's puns are lost, forces us to look again at that wordplay—which is precisely what wordplay invites us to do anyway—and reconsider whether it serves the triumph of enactment after all. In calling this writerly train of thought in the Sonnets "secondary," Booth implies that some other train of thought, presumably their empirical design as persuasion to love poetry or their mimetic design on representing the beauty of the youth, his worth, truth, or love, or perhaps those of the poet, is primary. But whatever primacy an empirical project may initially have held in the Sonnets, or may be maintained in such Elizabethan sonnet sequences as Spenser's or Sidney's, it has long since given way in Shakespeare's, first to the mimetic project so confidently proclaimed in Sonnet 55, and then to the exploration of the equivocal potential of poetry itself, which we have been tracing.

Shakespeare's primary concern seems to have shifted from the object to the process and medium of its representation, even to the point where the very capacity of his language to represent anything other than falsehood, betrayal, or "lying" will become an open and pressing question, particularly so, once the mimetic duplicity of the pun has been accepted. Yet Booth, attentive as he is to Shakespeare's ubiquitous wordplay and assiduous as he is in tracking down its connotations, is reluctant to grant it priority either as destroyer or preserver of mimetic effect. The puns are recognized as "there," but their importance is downplayed, precisely because their multiple meanings must be tracked down, and it is hard to know, once this preeminently *readerly* process is activated, where to stop.

For wordplay thrives in the dilated duration of response opened up by reading; hence it is a *writerly* device that demands our full *readerly* attention. Spoken puns we either catch or we don't; it is written puns we have the leisure and opportunity to go back to and retrace the trains of meaning they set in motion. Hence Joyce's remark that his ideal reader would devote a lifetime to his work. In this sense only, that the pun exists in the mode of afterthought, can its multiple meanings be thought of as secondary. Booth often remarks, in fact, on the way the flexibility of Elizabethan grammatical pointing works to serve multiple references and meanings. But so too does Elizabethan spelling. For it is the distinctive character of the pun that it enjoys its fullest expressive life in the written or printed, over and above the spoken, medium of language, and the relative freedom of Elizabethan orthography, its heterography as it were, plays directly into the writer's hands. Shakespeare's spelling of "tombe," for example, brings out its conflation of "tomb" and "tome" through the appended grapheme ("e") more forcibly to the eye than the sliding phoneme ("o") could to the ear, since the latter must be voiced one way or the other, much as the theatrical performance of a Shakespearean play must always generate a more limited field of meaning, by virtue of the interpretative options it must leave unexpressed, than the printed text.

The pun, by foregrounding its character as the privileged resource of writing, thus works against any notion of poetic enactment that presupposes the presence and immediacy of spoken language—hence Booth's quite traditional deprivileging of its effect—but at the same time it makes possible another kind of enactment beyond the reach of spoken language, with its hit-or-miss, here-and-gone rapidity, its momentary materiality. The relative transience, the short time available for the construction and concretization of meaning, in spoken as distinct from written wordplay, would thus seem to be a control upon its counter-enactive effect. But the written pun, by making available a longer, potentially endless, time for the construction of possible meanings, and hence the deconstruction of fixed or monumental meaning, reveals this control to be arbitrary and illusory, merely a momentary stay against multivocality. The overplus of time allowed by writing and reading for potentially endless construction and multiple concretization allows interpretation to do its deconstructive, fragmenting, counter-enactive work. The cultural authoritarianism that deprivileges or criminalizes wordplay in the attempt to save a univocal or unified reading is thus always a losing battle, a rearguard action fought against time in the name of a mimetic or supermimetic project that Shakespeare certainly states, in accordance with the poetic and rhetorical theory of his time, but also undermines and disowns as a function of his own writerly practice.

Chronology

1564	William Shakespeare born at Stratford-on-Avon to John Shakespeare, a butcher, and Mary Arden. He is baptized on April 26.
1582	Marries Anne Hathaway in November.
1583	Daughter Susanna born, baptized on May 26.
1585	Twins Hamnet and Judith born, baptized on February 2.
1588–90	Sometime during these years, Shakespeare goes to London, without family. First plays performed in London.
1590–92	*The Comedy of Errors*, the three parts of *Henry VI*.
1593–94	Publication of *Venus and Adonis* and *The Rape of Lucrece*, both dedicated to the Earl of Southampton. Shakespeare becomes a sharer in the Lord Chamberlain's company of actors. *The Taming of the Shrew, The Two Gentlemen of Verona, Richard III, Titus Andronicus*.
1595–97	*Romeo and Juliet, Richard II, King John, A Midsummer Night's Dream, Love's Labor's Lost*.
1596	Son Hamnet dies. Grant of arms to Shakespeare's father.
1597	*The Merchant of Venice, Henry IV, Part 1*. Purchases New Place in Stratford.
1598–1600	*Henry IV, Part 2, As You Like It, Much Ado about Nothing, Twelfth Night, The Merry Wives of Windsor, Henry V,* and *Julius Caesar*. Moves his company to the new Globe Theatre.
1601	*Hamlet*. Shakespeare's father dies, buried on September 8.
1601–2	*Troilus and Cressida*.

133

1603	Death of Queen Elizabeth; James VI of Scotland becomes James I of England; Shakespeare's company becomes the King's Men.
1603–4	*All's Well That Ends Well, Measure for Measure, Othello.*
1605–6	*King Lear, Macbeth.*
1607	Marriage of daughter Susanna on June 5.
1607–8	*Timon of Athens, Antony and Cleopatra, Pericles, Coriolanus.*
1608	Shakespeare's mother dies, buried on September 9.
1609	*Cymbeline,* publication of sonnets. Shakespeare's company purchases Blackfriars Theatre.
1610–11	*The Winter's Tale, The Tempest.* Shakespeare retires to Stratford.
1612–13	*Henry VIII, The Two Noble Kinsmen.*
1616	Marriage of daughter Judith on February 10. Shakespeare dies at Stratford on April 23.
1623	Publication of the Folio edition of Shakespeare's plays.

Contributors

HAROLD BLOOM, Sterling Professor of the Humanities at Yale University, is the author of *The Anxiety of Influence, Poetry and Repression*, and many other volumes of literary criticism. His forthcoming study, *Freud: Transference and Authority*, attempts a full-scale reading of all of Freud's major writings. A MacArthur Prize Fellow, he is general editor of five series of literary criticism published by Chelsea House. During 1987–88, he was appointed Charles Eliot Norton Professor of Poetry at Harvard University.

C. L. BARBER, Professor of Literature at the University of California, Santa Barbara, is the author of *Shakespeare's Festive Comedy, The Form of Faustus' Fortunes*, and *The Lyric and Dramatic Milton*.

ROSALIE L. COLIE was Professor of English at Brown University until her death in 1972. She is the author of *Paradoxia Epidemica: The Resources of Kind, Shakespeare's Living Art*, and a book of poems, *Atlantic Wall and Other Poems*.

STEPHEN BOOTH, Professor of English at the University of California, Berkeley, is the author of *An Essay on Shakespeare's Sonnets, The Book Called Holinshed's Chronicles* and *King Lear, Macbeth, Indefinition, and Tragedy* and the editor of *Shakespeare's Sonnets*.

THOMAS M. GREENE, Chairman of Comparative Literature at Yale University, is the author of *The Descent from Heaven, Rabelais: A Study in Comic Courage, The Light in Troy*, and a book of essays, *The Vulnerable Text*.

HOWARD FELPERIN is Professor of English at Melbourne University,

Australia. His books include *Shakespearean Romance, Shakespearean Representation,* and *Beyond Deconstruction: The Uses and Abuses of Literary Theory.*

Bibliography

Baldwin, T. W. *On the Literary Genetics of Shakespeare's Poems and Sonnets*. Urbana: University of Illinois Press, 1951.

Bradbrook, Muriel C. "The Fashioning of a Courtier." In *Shakespeare and Elizabethan Poetry*, 141–61. London: Chatto & Windus, 1951.

Cruttwell, Patrick. "A Reading of the Sonnets." *The Hudson Review* 5 (1953): 554–70.

———. *The Shakespearean Moment and Its Place in the Poetry of the Seventeenth Century*. New York: Columbia University Press, 1955.

De Grazia, Margreta. "Babbling Will in *Shake-speares Sonnets* 127 to 154." In *Spenser Studies: A Renaissance Poetry Annual I,* edited by Patrick Cullen and Thomas P. Roche, Jr., 121–34. Pittsburgh: University of Pittsburgh Press, 1980.

———. "Shakespeare's View of Language: An Historical Perspective." *Shakespeare Quarterly* 29 (1978): 374–88.

Empson, William. *Seven Types of Ambiguity*. London: Chatto & Windus, 1930.

Graves, Robert and Laura Riding. "A Study in Original Punctuation and Spelling." In *The Common Asphodel*, 84–95. London: Hamish Hamilton, 1949.

Greene, Thomas M. "Anti-hermeneutics: The Case of Shakespeare's Sonnet 129." In *Poetic Traditions of the English Renaissance,* edited by Maynard Mack and George deForest Lord, 143–61. New Haven: Yale University Press, 1982.

Herrnstein, Barbara, ed. *Discussions of Shakespeare's Sonnets*. Boston: Heath, 1964.

Hotson, Leslie. *Shakespeare's Sonnets Dated, and Other Essays*. London: Rupert Hart-Davis, 1949.

Hubler, Edward. *The Sense of Shakespeare's Sonnets*. Princeton University Studies in English, no. 33. Princeton: Princeton University Press, 1952.

Hubler, Edward, Northrop Frye, L. A. Fiedler, Stephen Spender, and R. P. Blackmur, eds. *The Riddle of Shakespeare's Sonnets*. New York: Basic Books, 1962.

Hunter, G. K. "The Dramatic Technique of Shakespeare's Sonnets." *Essays in Criticism* 3 (1953): 152–64.

Jakobson, Roman, and Lawrence G. Jones. *Shakespeare's Verbal Art in "Th' Expense of Spirit."* De Propreitatibus Litterarum, Series Practica, no. 35. The Hague: Mouton, 1970.

Krieger, Murray. "The Innocent Insinuations of Wit: The Strategy of Language in Shakespeare's Sonnets." In *The Play and Place of Criticism,* 19–36. Baltimore: The Johns Hopkins University Press, 1967.

————. *A Window to Criticism: Shakespeare's Sonnets and Modern Poetics*. Princeton: Princeton University Press, 1964.

Landry, Hilton. *Interpretations in Shakespeare's Sonnets*. Perspectives in Criticism, no. 14. Berkeley and Los Angeles: University of California Press, 1963.

Lanham, Richard. *The Motives of Eloquence: Literary Rhetoric in the Renaissance*. New Haven: Yale University Press, 1976.

Leishman, J. B. *Themes and Variations in Shakespeare's Sonnets*. New York: Harper & Row, 1966.

Lever, J. W. "Shakespeare." In *The Elizabethan Love Sonnet*, 162–272. London: Methuen, 1956.

Martin, Philip J. *Shakespeare's Sonnets: Self, Love and Art*. Cambridge: Cambridge University Press, 1972.

Melchiori, Giorgio. *Shakespeare's Dramatic Meditations: An Experiment in Criticism*. Oxford: Clarendon, 1976.

Mizener, Arthur. "The Structure of Figurative Language in Shakespeare's Sonnets." *The Southern Review* 5 (1940): 730–47.

Muir, Kenneth. *Shakespeare's Sonnets*. London: Allen & Unwin, 1979.

Nowottny, Winifred M. T. "Formal Elements in Shakespeare's Sonnets I–VI." *Essays in Criticism* 2 (1952): 76–84.

Pequigney, Joseph. *Such Is My Love: A Study of Shakespeare's Sonnets*. Chicago: University of Chicago Press, 1985.

Prince, F. T. *The Poems*. The Arden Edition of the Works of William Shakespeare. London: Methuen, 1960.

Ramsey, Paul. *The Fickle Glass: A Study of Shakespeare's Sonnets*. AMS Studies in the Renaissance, no. 4. New York: AMS, 1979.

Ransom, John Crowe. "Shakespeare at Sonnets." *The Southern Review* 3 (1938): 531–53.

Regan, Mariann Sanders. "Shakespeare's Sonnets." In *Love Words: The Self and the Text in Medieval and Renaissance Poetry*, 223–54. Ithaca: Cornell University Press, 1982.

Rosmarin, Adena. "Hermeneutics vs. Erotics: Shakespeare's *Sonnets* and Interpretive History." *PMLA* 100 (1985): 20–37.

Rowse, A. L. *Shakespeare's Sonnets: The Problems Solved*. 2d ed. New York: Harper & Row, 1973.

————. *Shakespeare the Man*. New York: Harper & Row, 1973.

Sedgwick, Eve Kosofsky. "Swan in Love: The Example of Shakespeare's Sonnets." In *Between Men: English Literature and Male Homosocial Desire*. New York: Columbia University Press, 1985.

Shakespeare, William. *Shakespeare's Sonnets,* edited by Stephen Booth. New Haven: Yale University Press, 1977.

Stirling, Brents. *The Shakespeare Sonnet Order: Poems and Groups*. Berkeley: University of California Press, 1968.

Wait, R. J. C. *The Background to Shakespeare's Sonnets*. London: Chatto & Windus, 1972.

Wilde, Oscar. "The Portrait of Mr. W. H." *Blackwood's Edinburgh Magazine* 146 (1889): 1–21.

Wilson, John Dover. *An Introduction to the Sonnets of Shakespeare for the Use of Historians and Others.* Cambridge: Cambridge University Press, 1963.

Winny, James. *The Master-Mistress: A Study of Shakespeare's Sonnets.* London: Chatto & Windus, 1968.

Acknowledgments

"An Essay on Shakespeare's Sonnets" (originally entitled "Introduction") by C. L. Barber from *The Laurel Shakespeare: The Sonnets* by C. L. Barber, © 1960 by Western Printing and Lithographing Co. Reprinted by permission.

"Criticism and the Analysis of Craft: The Sonnets" by Rosalie L. Colie from *Shakespeare's Living Art* by Rosalie L. Colie, © 1974 by Princeton University Press. Reprinted by permission of Princeton University Press.

"Commentaries on the Sonnets" by Stephen Booth from *Shakespeare's Sonnets,* edited by Stephen Booth, © 1977 by Yale University. Reprinted by permission of Yale University Press.

"Pitiful Thrivers: Failed Husbandry in the Sonnets" by Thomas M. Greene from *Shakespeare and the Question of Theory,* edited by Patricia Parker and Geoffrey H. Hartman, © 1985 by Thomas M. Greene. Reprinted by permission of the author and Methuen & Co., Ltd.

"Toward a Poststructuralist Practice: A Reading of Shakespeare's Sonnets" by Howard Felperin from *Beyond Deconstruction: The Uses and Abuses of Literary Theory* by Howard Felperin, © 1985 by Howard Felperin. Reprinted by permission.

Index